How To Pinstripe

How To Pinstripe

MOTORBOOKS

This book is dedicated to my Lord and Savior Jesus Christ,
for giving me imagination and the gifts to express it.
And to my loving wife Judy, who encouraged
and supported me to reach further than my dreams.

First published in 2007 by Motorbooks, an imprint of MBI Publishing Company LLC, Galtier Plaza, Suite 200, 380 Jackson Street, St. Paul, MN 55101 USA

Motorbooks titles are also available at discounts in bulk quantity for industrial or sales-promotional use. For details write to Special Sales Manager at MBI Publishing Company, Galtier Plaza, Suite 200, 380 Jackson Street, St. Paul, MN 55101 USA.

To find out more about our books, join us online at www.motorbooks.com.

Johnson, Alan, 1946-
  How to pinstripe / by Alan "AJ" Johnson.
    p. cm.
  Includes index.
  ISBN-13: 978-0-7603-2749-4 (softbound)
  ISBN-10: 0-7603-2749-1 (softbound)
  1. Automobiles—Decoration. 2. Pinstriping of motor vehicles. I. Title.
  TL255.2.J64 2007
  629.28'72—dc22

                    2007006298

Front and back cover: Author Alan "AJ" Johnson is the guy today's top collectors turn to when they're looking for period-authentic restorations of the most historically significant hot rods out there . . . like the famed Berardini Bros. "404 Jr." 1932 Ford roadster owned by Roger Morrison. No less a towering kustom culture figure than Von Dutch laid the original lines on this beauty back in 1953. In addition to top-notch advice for beginning and veteran stripers alike, inside this book Johnson relates what it was like to get inside the head of the "Father of Modern Pinstriping" in order to recreate his lines on the Berardini car.

Title pages: Johnson puts the finishing touches on the headlight bucket of a Model A Ford roadster pickup.

About the Author
Alan "AJ" Johnson caught the pinstriping bug at age 11, when his father took him to see Ed "Big Daddy" Roth at the New York Coliseum. After graduating from Newark School of Fine Industrial Art in 1968, Alan landed a job as art director at a New York City ad agency. In 1974 he moved his family to the country and started his own business, which still thrives today. Alan is also a consultant for automotive paint manufacturers and the author of several how-to articles for trade periodicals. He has taught and demonstrated his pinstriping techniques throughout the United States, United Kingdom, and Finland. He recently launched his own line of signature brushes with The Mack Brush Company. Alan also offers his own limited edition prints of this unique American art form. Please visit www.johnsongrafix.com.

Editor: Dennis Pernu
Designer: Kou Lor

Printed in China

CONTENTS

ACKNOWLEDGMENTS

This book was made possible by the generous help and support of these fine people and companies, and by the trust of my loyal customers whose vehicles appear throughout these pages. Special thanks to Carol Mittelsdorf for her organizational skills, patience, and friendship:

1-Shot paint
Bill Beckner
Dave Crouse
DeWayne Connot
Rich Fass
Jon and Chris Fast, Mack Brush Company
Robert Genat
Dave Hightower
Christopher Johnson
Eric and Joanna Johnson
Ralph Marano
Carol Mittelsdrof
Roger Morrison
Russ Mowry
Skipp Phelps
Bill Riedel, Sr.
Ed Roth
Glenn Smith
T. J. Ronan Paint Corp
Robert Turnquist
Clay White

Special thanks, also to all my "pinhead" brethren, who freely give their time and talents, volunteering to support the many charities that are dear to me:

Children's Hospital of Wisconsin, www.chw.org
Make-A-Wish Foundation, www.wish.org
Rainbow Connection, www.rainbowwishconnection.org
Two Kids Foundation, www.twokidsfoundation.org

FOREWORD
By Roger Morrison

In my opinion, a great pinstriper is like a sensitive piano accompanist for a solo vocalist. The pianist supports and enhances the soloist's performance without calling undue attention to him or herself. As a consummate pinstriper, Alan Johnson enhances and complements the design of the automobile without calling undue attention to the actual pinstriping. In both the musical and automotive examples, the sum of the two parts working together is greater than the whole.

Because of his quiet and unassuming nature, Alan's name may not be as widely known as other practitioners of the delicate art. No bizarre antics, tantrums, or tirades. Happily, his focus, energy, and talent flow from his brush rather than from his mouth. Also unlike some artists, Alan is a willing and proactive teacher. I have seen him personally encourage young pinstripers at auto shows.

Those of us fortunate enough to either see or own a car pinstripped by Alan enjoy the great benefit of witnessing the work of a genuine master.

It is my great good fortune to call Alan a friend. I have willingly and happily turned several cars over to him for the pinstriping, saying, "Use your own good judgment." In each case the result was more than I could have conceived and better than I could have imagined.

Now the reader of this seminal instruction book has the opportunity to embark on an exciting new time of self-discovery and skill-building. As you delve into this book, I know you will be challenged and inspired.

Go for it!

Pat Berardini and Roger Morrison with the famed Berardini Bros. "404 Jr." roadster.

INTRODUCTION

QUESTION: How do you learn how to pinstripe?
ANSWER: Get one gallon of 1-Shot lettering paint and three or four pinstriping brushes. When you get to the bottom of the can, you'll know how to pinstripe.

Having been asked to write a book on the subject, I searched the back pages of my mind and found a memory of me as a 12-year-old kid at a car show at the New York Coliseum, where for the first time I saw a hot rod being pinstriped, and by the master himself: Ed "Big Daddy" Roth. I was mystified by his palette, the can of paint with the arrow and bulls-eye on it, and exotic brush he was using.

I thought to myself, so that's how it's done. Armed with little more than a desire to attempt this unusual type of painting, I set out in search of the materials I witnessed Ed Roth using to bring my dream of painting hot rods to life. Who knew that some 30 years later, Ed would be sending people to have their cars striped by me at a car show? He was a great guy.

I grew up outside of the small town of Red Bank, New Jersey, and saw very few cars with pinstriping on them, let alone anyone actually pinstriping a car in person. With many questions in my head, I sought out the only information available to me at the time, which came from a few small

This is the way I learned to pinstripe: 1 gallon of paint and a few brushes. If you have the hunger and the desire to triumph over the unknown, you will get to the bottom of the can. If you never really wanted to learn and you give up halfway through the can, you are only out the price of a can of paint and a few brushes. You can always pass them on to the kid down the street.

"The little books," as we called them, were full of hard-to-see striping photos, but they were about all a kid in River Plaza, New Jersey, could find about pinstriping. I would fall asleep reading those magazines as headlights raced across my bedroom walls.

rod and custom magazines with even smaller pictures of dashboards covered in cool-looking lines.

After much searching, I bought a brush in a wallpaper and paint store and I started painting everything in sight. Little knowledge is not necessarily a bad thing, I tested the limits of everything that brush could and could not do. Trial and error *is* the best teacher. Since I didn't know I couldn't stripe, I just did it.

My goal with this book is to lift the veil of mystery that has surrounded pinstriping for the beginner and eliminate the fear of learning to pinstripe. Hopefully, car enthusiasts will find it entertaining. Veteran pinstripers

might find a few new insights to make their jobs a little more enjoyable.

I hope to introduce you to all the materials and methods you may need to get to "the bottom of the can." There are as many ways to pinstripe as there are brushes and pinstripers who hold them. The brother- and sisterhood of fellow artists ("pinheads") have graciously shared their own knowledge and techniques with me, adding up to numerous years of experience that I now will share with you.

But remember: you will have to see what works for you. About halfway through the can you will know. So just get the brush and let's go!

CHAPTER 1
A UNIQUE AMERICAN ART FORM

There are many theories about when pinstripes were first laid down as decoration. Some say the Egyptian chariots were highly decorated with pinstriping. I'll let the experts squabble over which theory is correct.

This is how I imagine it all began. Pinstriping started soon after the invention of the wheel. The guy with the second set of wheels didn't want to be second-class, so he found a guy in a cave who had chewed roots into soft fibers that he then used to decorate his walls with paints made from berries. This unusual fellow with the chewed roots decorated this second-class set of wheels into the first custom wheels. Soon all the other cave dwellers were lining up to get their rides to look cooler than the last. Chewing roots into a crude brush had its drawbacks, though. It seems that the roots contained some kind of hallucinogenic that left this artist staring into space for hours at a time. Soon, work piled up that he never got around to finishing. The people waiting got tired of all the excuses; they found another guy living down by the river who was famous for hunting sabertooth squirrels. He also was known for painting cool designs with a stick that had squirrel hair tied to the end. And so the first good brush without side effects was born.

The dust of time passed with numerous other experiments, which led to further developments in the wheel, pigments, and paint technology. Stone gave way to wood-spoked wheels. Carriage ornamentation and coach lining boomed during the Victorian Era. This new prosperity and opulence had neighbors once again trying to outshine each other. This "Carriage Era" was a time of unprecedented development. Carriage manufacturing was at its peak. A variety of ornamentation and decoration was painted onto each and every machine that existed during this time. Also, paint and varnish manufacturers broadened their palettes and developed more durable colors. The demand for ornamentation also moved some "stripers," as they were now called, to experiment and refine their striping "pencils," as they were called during

Thanks to a slew of articles published in enthusiast magazines, 1954–1955 is sometimes cited as a watershed period for pinstriping. The March 1955 issue of *Rod & Custom*, with George Barris' heavily "Dutched" 1949 Ford woody on the cover, also included a how-to feature with step-by-step photos that showcased the striping talents of Art Summers.

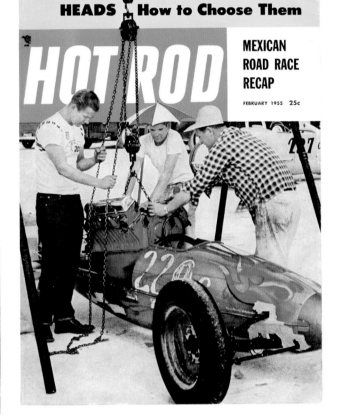

Other pinstriping features that appeared in hot rodding magazines during late 1954 and early 1955 included a piece about Jack Chrisman's Von Dutch–striped '29 Tudor in the December 1954 issue of *HOT ROD* (left) that was followed two months later by Bob D'Olivo's article, "Camel's Hair Capers," in the same publication. The cover of that issue (right) featured an Eric Rickman Ektachrome of the Reed Bros./Leroy Neumayer belly-tank lakester, which had been flamed and striped by Von Dutch.

this time. The hair of choice for these new brushes was, you guessed it, squirrel! The highest designing and artistic standards were developed by respected artists such as, Fred Weber, S. H. Redmond, and others. Safes, wagons, omni-buses, streetcars, and railroad coaches all became works of art adorned in scrollwork as the horse slowly gave way to horsepower.

The horseless carriage was just that—some looked as if engines were retrofitted to existing carriages. Therefore, the art form of pinstriping carried over without much change. But vehicle ornamentation slowly declined to just coach lining until the 1950s, when some guy playing a flute and painting crazy designs, along with some other colorful characters in California, decided to open the paint box again.

Although some believe he invented a line of designer caps and T-shirts, Kenneth "Von Dutch" Howard was the self-proclaimed originator of "modern pinstriping." His freeform style is still seen today. Many other pioneers like Ed "Big Daddy" Roth, Dean Jeffries, and Tommy "The Greek" Hrones, to name just a few, also helped popularize pinstriping. Again, I'll let the experts argue over who did what first. I'm just truly thankful that this art form is still to this day loved and enjoyed for what it is. Oh . . . I'm also thankful for squirrels.

GARAGE TO GALLERY WALLS

The "kustom" culture enjoyed pinstriping for decades, without really realizing that it really is art. But I don't think it would make a bit of difference if pinstriping were awarded the badge of "real" art by some art critic. Just as that social outcast, the hot rod, slowly found acceptance in society as the more sophisticated "street rod," pinstriping—one "lowbrow" art form

Ed "Big Daddy" Roth signed my striping kit at a car show in 1992. On it, he wrote, "Follow the Spirit." What a weekend we had, sharing stories that ranged from General Motors to theology. I was thrilled to finally have the chance to meet him and tell him the story of our first encounter at the New York Coliseum when I was a lad of 12. He was a major inspiration for me as I learned to paint.

from the hot rod world—is gaining appreciation as a uniquely American art form.

While many automotive pinstriping artists have had our art displayed in galleries and at shows, most of us would rather see our artwork viewed on the "gallery of the road." Turning heads and nods of approval always bring a feeling of satisfaction. Without searching too deeply for the underlying reasons, I think the art world today is made up by and for people with serious psychological problems.

The automotive society first started collecting art in the 1950s. Today, just look at auction results, notably from the Brucker auction held in May 2006 at the Peterson Museum.

Kustom culture gallery auctions are not the only place to find hot rod art. "Real" art galleries from coast to coast are beginning to accept art that pioneers like Von Dutch, Roth, and Robert Williams popularized. An entirely new

demographic is beginning to appreciate the art we have enjoyed for years. Today, almost every major auto show hosts a pinstriping jam, after which a sale or auction of the resulting artwork takes place. Terry Cook—promoter of Lead East, the "World's Biggest '50s Party"—had the foresight to offer one of the first gallery settings for artists to demonstrate and sell pinstriping. Auctions held at this event have raised thousands of dollars for children's charities in the past years. Many collectors seek out these types of shows, in order to purchase these pieces of artwork that several artists have worked on.

Annually, artists continue taking pinstriping to new levels of perfection at more and more automotive and pinhead events. And crucial to pinstriping's growing popularity and further development, new artists are learning new ideas and techniques from older pinstripers who freely give time and priceless information gleaned over years of trial and error.

CHAPTER 2
PAINT, PRODUCTS, AND COLOR THEORY

The first time I saw Ed "Big Daddy" Roth, I watched with amazement as his giant hands worked that tiny brush back and forth on a magazine palette. I had no idea who this wild-looking character was, completely clad in hand-painted, airbrushed attire and wearing his signature top hat. I was mesmerized by the way he went about his work, with steady concentration exuding tons of contagious joy.

That magical can of paint, with an arrow and bull's-eye logo, sat on his palette. Every time I see a 1-Shot label or smell the paint, I'm reminded of that encounter so many

years ago, watching Ed Roth pinstriping at the legendary New York Coliseum Car Show.

Known for its good coverage and high gloss, 1-Shot Lettering Enamel has been the paint of choice for sign-painters and pinstripers for many years. Today, with input from signwriters and stripers, 1-Shot offers a wide range of colors and reducers made for all types of weather conditions.

Ronan Lettering Enamel is another good paint for striping. Most stripers have both of these brands in their kits, and for many years each manufacturer has been a great supporter of

1-Shot enamel has been around ever since I can remember. It is named, appropriately, for the way it covers—in one "shot." Additives help the paint to dry harder, which makes it more durable. Enamels can be clear-coated by adding hardener to the enamel, followed by a light sealer coat of clear before the finish clear coat is applied. Using high-temperature reducer made for working in hot weather will keep the paint wetter longer, while a low-temperature reducer evaporates more quickly so the paint will dry faster in cooler weather.

Ronan Lettering Enamel is quality paint available in a good range of colors. I especially like the reds. You will find both the Ronan and 1-Shot brands in many sign-painters' kits, as there are differences in the colors and coverage. Both 1-Shot and Ronan have been very generous over the years in their support of painters, donating paints to letterhead and pinhead gatherings all over the world.

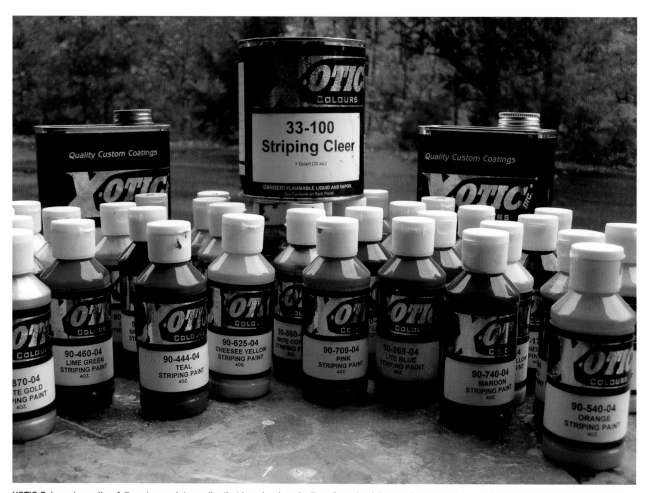

XOTIC Colours is another full custom-paint supplier that has developed a line of good striping urethanes and high- to low-temperature reducers that make these quick-drying paints easier to control. XOTIC has a wide range of colors, pearls, and metallic paints that cover well. I believe that for durability reasons, urethane paint will become more and more popular as stripers become accustomed to using it.

The Alsa Corporation, a full custom-paint supplier, has introduced a striping urethane to its line of products. Stripers have been requesting a good striping urethane for years and this is one of them.

letterheads and pinheads at gatherings all over the world. Ronan offers a complete line of colors and paint products and has a great selection of reds that I like and which cover well.

To comply with government regulations, some ingredients, such as lead, have been removed or substituted. Hardeners have been added to lend durability to the paint. Some stripers use automotive reducers (known as *hot reducers* in the trade) to make these paints perform the way they want. However, some hot reducers tend to break down the chemical makeup of the paint, so glossy paints may flatten out or become dull prematurely. Play it safe: stick with the reducers provided by the paint manufacturers.

Kustom Shop, a new company that clearly has the graphic artist in mind, offers a modified alkyd enamel designed to provide excellent hiding, superior flow, high gloss, durability, and faster drying time than traditional striping enamels. The EZ-Flow line includes many new vibrant colors, plus a variety of low-luster hues that are great for striping suede paint jobs. EZ-Flow striping and lettering hardener, mid- and high-temperature reducers, and brush-preserving oil finish off this quality line nicely. I recommend you try all of these brands to see which works best for you.

There have been several attempts to produce a quality, water-based lettering and striping paint. Not many manufactures have had any success promoting them in today's professional market. Because natural-fiber brushes have *continued on page 18*

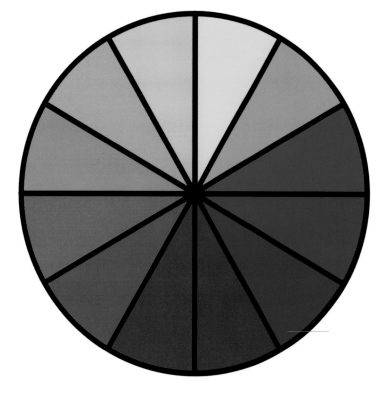

For a few dollars, you can pick up a cheap color wheel in almost any store that has a craft section. This chart is a priceless tool for anyone serious about any type of artwork. To me, color is the most valuable concept in the design process. Your color selection will make the difference between a good job and a great job. There are plenty of books available about color theory, and the more you learn about color, the more there will be to know. The basic information on a color wheel should be enough to get you out of a tight spot when you get stumped on a striping color.

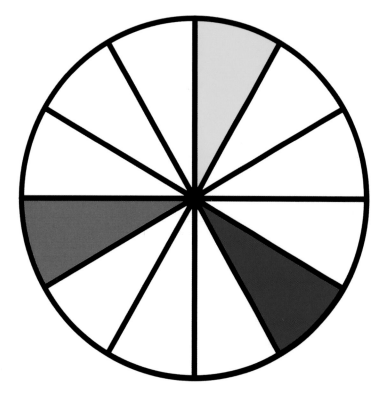

Red, blue, and yellow are primary colors, by which all other colors can be made.

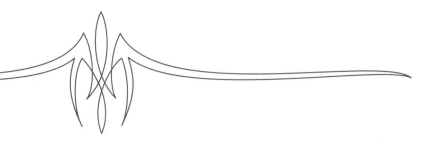

Orange, violet, and green are secondary colors, which are created by combining any two primary colors in equal intensity.

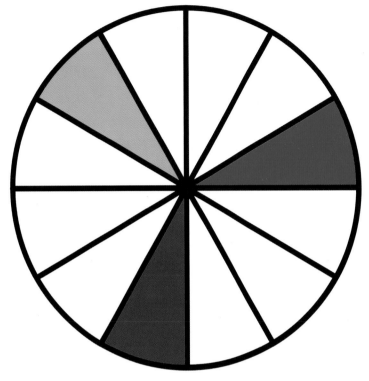

Intermediary colors (yellow-green, blue-green, etc.) are created by varying the percentage of the primary and secondary colors that are mixed together.

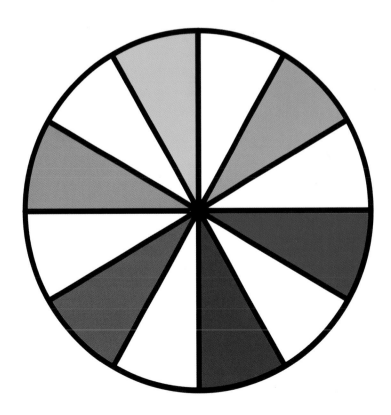

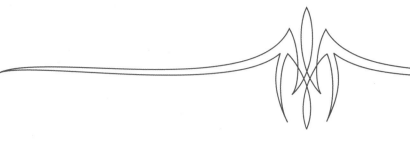

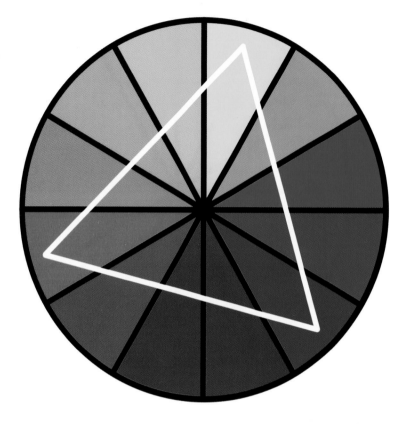

Triadic harmonies are any three colors forming a triangle on the color wheel.

continued from page 15
"bad-hair days" when soaked in water-based paints (certainly not a favorite pastime of our friends, the squirrels), manufacturers have attempted to develop synthetic brushes that work well with these products. I have tried these paints and brushes and found they do not perform with any reliable degree.

Lately, striping with urethanes has been gaining popularity for a number of good reasons. They dry quickly, so you can work fast, and they are more durable in the long run. For years, some stripers have used single-stage urethanes produced by DuPont, PPG, and other automotive paint brands. House of Kolor has added more colors over the years to keep up with the demands of the ever-widening custom-paint business.

I do not recommend urethanes for beginners; they are not as forgiving as enamels. Because of their quick-drying nature, they take a little more time to get used to. Urethanes are, however, great for striping when you plan to spray a clear topcoat over your striping. Because of urethane's durability, there's no need to worry about *lifting* problems that can occur when you clear-coat over enamel.

Alsa Corporation, XOTIC Colours, and others have been developing urethane striping product lines with good arrays of colors, including premixed metallics and pearls, plus clears that can be used to create custom blends by adding powdered metallics, pearls, and even metalflakes. The coverage of these products is very good as well.

COLOR THEORY

Basic color theory could fill volumes of books, but as far as we are concerned with vehicle pinstriping, a basic understanding should get you out of the woods. The following is a summary of the rules that you should be aware of when you approach a vehicle-striping project. I encourage you to investigate color theory more deeply if you wish to pursue a serious profession in pinstriping. The more you know, the better you will become.

Isaac Newton discovered the *color spectrum* in the 1600s. He taught us that light equals color. The visible color spectrum consists of red, orange, yellow, green, blue, indigo, and violet.

Without getting our brains tangled up, try thinking of the visible color spectrum as a pie and each color of the

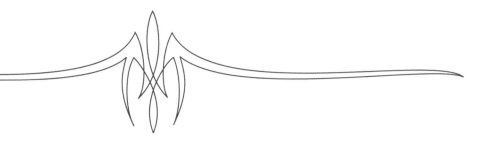

Tetrad or double complements are any four colors forming a rectangle or square on the color wheel.

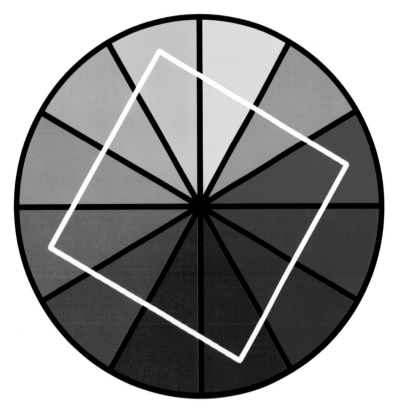

spectrum as a slice of the pie. Red, blue, and yellow are *primary colors*, from which all other colors can be made. Orange, violet, and green are *secondary colors*, which are created by combining any two primary colors in equal intensity. *Intermediary colors* are created by varying the percentage of the primary and secondary colors that are mixed together (yellow-green, blue-green, etc.). The result is 12 *hues* that make up a traditional color wheel.

Complementary colors are colors opposite each other on the color wheel, i.e., red and green, yellow and violet, and blue and orange. These are said to complement each other or work well together.

Here are some basic color rules to memorize:

- Neutral gray is the result of mixing equal parts of any two complementary colors.
- Adding white to any hue makes a *tint*.
- Adding black to any hue makes a *shade*.
- Adding white *and* black makes *tones* of any hue.

- *Triadic harmonies* are any three colors forming a triangle on the color wheel.
- *Tetrad* or *double complements* are any four colors forming a rectangle or square on the color wheel.

Color affects us in many different ways. Green gives many people a sense of serenity. Orange represents joy and sunshine. Subtle colors calm us; stronger, intense colors stimulate us; pastels seem delicate, and deep, rich colors look and feel luxurious. Visually, *warm* colors (red, orange, and yellow) advance; *cooler* colors (blue and green) recede; light colors make objects look larger, and dark colors make the same objects look smaller.

That's enough for now, we can keep going forever, but it's time to paint. Because color is so important to me, we will discuss color theory again throughout the book. Just remember that a well-thought-out color combination complements any automotive restoration job.

CHAPTER 3
TOOLS

BRUSHES

In 1891 Andrew Mack, an accomplished carriage striper, became frustrated with the quality of brushes available at the time and set out to make his own. Today, hand-tied Mack brushes are still made to the same specifications as they were back in the 1800s.

Today, pinstriping brushes are available in a wide variety of styles and sizes to fit any type of pinstriping need. In the past, stripers made their own "striping pencils," as they were called, from a portion of a larger camel hair brush. Incidentally, "camel hair" brushes get their name from their inventor, one Mr. Camel; they do not and never have consisted of camel hair, which is woolly and would be unsuitable for the purpose. Instead, the hair often comes from the tail of a squirrel. Blue squirrel is the most readily available. These hairs are very soft and are available in long lengths. Before manufacturers took up striping brushes, the hair was manipulated into the desirable shape by twisting it between the forefinger and thumb.

Some pinstripers still customize larger brushes to suit their needs, often trimming down or retying the hair to make smaller or shorter brushes. The first pinstriping brush I ever found was made in the Dominican Republic in sizes 00 and 0. The little paint and wallpaper store where I bought them also carried sign-painting quills in various sizes. These "Old Dominicans," as we called them, were excellent for straight lines and also worked well for designs. The Mack Brush Company offers brushes designed with the input of professional stripers that should fill any striping situation, from the finest thin line to the most intricate scrollwork.

Many types of brushes are available to suit any type of decorative painting you can imagine. A few other manufacturers in addition to Mack also are making great strides to keep up with the demand for variety and quality.

This fine scrollwork in gold leaf with tiny details by Dave Hightower is a fine example of the need for a variety of good quality brushes.

BRUSH CHOICES

Here are some pinstriping brushes offered by the Mack Brush Company, from left to right:

1. **Broadliners** *(sizes 00 to 7)*, as their name implies, are adapted for broad lines. The brush size (00 to 7) determines the width of the line. Used on its edge, each size makes a slightly narrower line than when used flat. Also make great fill-in brushes for wide graphics.

2. **Dagger Stripers** *(sizes 00 to 4)* are tapered to a point on both top and bottom. This shape gives the brush a more flexible characteristic. Great for outlining flames.

3. **Series 10 Sword Stripers** *(sizes 000 to 4)* are Mack's original sword striping brushes. These are good, reliable all-around brushes for lines and design. Still hand-crafted and shaped as they were many years ago.

4. **Series 20 Automotive Touch-up Brushes** *(sizes 00 to5)* are commonly found in auto-supply stores. A slightly stiffer blend than the Series 10.

5. Available from Mack, the **XCaliber Stripers** *(size 0000 to 0)* have shorter hair lengths than the Series 10, just 1 1/2 inches compared to the average 2 and 2 1/4 inches. This shorter hair length allows greater control for intricate designs.

6. The **Series 75** *(sizes 00 to 1)* are synthetic stripers that can be used with water-based and urethane paint. Designed for straight lines.

7. **Mach-One Series 101 Stripers** *(sizes 00 to 2)* are fashioned after the Grumbacher 1010 striper but with a round handle.

8. **Mack-Lite Stripers** *(sizes 00 to 2)* are the stripers with less belly. The shape is similar to the "Old Dominicans" that were discontinued several years ago. Made with Kazan squirrel hair and bound with a brass ferrule. Length out is graduated from 1 5/8 to 2 inches.

9. **Mack-Belly Stripers** *(sizes 00 to 2)* are exactly like Mack-Lite Stripers, only with more belly to the shape to carry more paint. Also made with Kazan squirrel hair.

10. **Fast-Lite Stripers** *(sizes 00 to 2)* are similar to Mack-Lite Stripers, but with longer hairs from blue squirrels. Length out is graduated from 1 7/8 to 2 1/4 inches.

11. The **Series 70** *(sizes 00 to 2)* are made much like the Fast-Lite Stripers, but with mixed hair to give the brush more body. For use with water-based paint, which has a higher density. For body and snap, the fibers are a mix of the synthetic filament Taklon and squirrel. Thegenerous amount of squirrel hair helps carry enough paint. These make great outdoor stripers on windy days because they hold their body and shape.

12. The DeWayne Connot **DC Flat Liners Series 1310** *(sizes 00 to 1)* are designed for long lines. The squirrel hair comes from China and is softer than the traditional Siberian squirrel hair. It's also the same hair used in Series 10 brushes.

13. **Glawson/Mack Extra Long Stripers** *(sizes 00 and 0)* are shaped like Fast-Lite Stripers. Both sizes have a hair length out of 2 inches, but this striper can be used with either lettering enamel or urethane paint. Great for long lines.

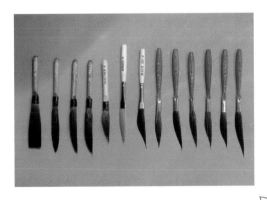

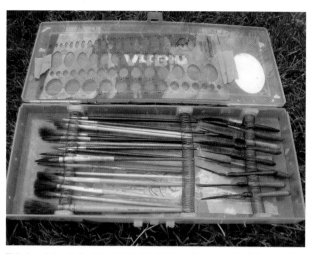

This brush box is just the right size for traveling around with enough brushes to do most anything that comes along. I just pop it into my luggage and when I reach my destination I find paint at the nearest sign supplier.

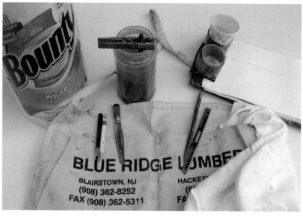

This is a basic kit that you can quickly rig up from simple household items. With a little imagination, you can find plenty of substitutes. It's always an adventure, you know, and necessity is the mother of invention.

STRIPING KIT

I've been striping for over 40 years now, and am blessed with a wonderful studio full of everything I need to do any job that rolls in. But I still work out of my portable paint kit, whether I'm in the studio or on the road. Over the years I've stored my supplies in everything from ammunition boxes to milk crates and metal toolboxes of many sizes. When traveling by plane, I carry a small box with a variety of brushes that I may need to do most anything.

THE BASIC STRIPING KIT

Keep a kit stocked with these basic items and you will be ready for most any striping task:

- Wax and grease remover (1 quart)
- Denatured alcohol (1 pint)
- Paint in primary colors, plus black and white (half-pints)
- Reducer for hot and cold conditions
- Mineral spirits (1 gallon for brush washing)
- Paper towels (Bounty towels have no lint)
- Clipboard and magazine for a palette
- Palette stand or table
- Metal double 3-ounce cup holder
- 3-ounce paper cups (non-waxed)
- Brushes in a brush box
- Ice-cube or small baking tray for brush-soaking
- Palette knife or craft sticks for paint-mixing
- 3/4-inch and 1/4-inch masking tape
- 1/4-inch and 1/8-inch Scotch Fine Line tape
- Small container of baby powder
- Olfa snap-off blade knife
- Stabilo pencils (white and blue)
- Saral wax-free transfer paper (1 roll each of white and blue)
- Apron
- Flexible clear plastic ruler or yard stick
- Sketchpad

Striping paint is available from sign suppliers almost anywhere, or you can have it shipped to wherever you are going since it is impossible to carry paint and other flammable liquids with you onboard a plane these days.

When I was at the Hot Rod Reunion in Bakersfield, California, I had striped and lettered a car that was on display in the lobby of the host hotel. The car had been slightly damaged in transport and needed some touching up. Within 5 miles of the event, I found all the supplies I needed. Like someone said, "Keep it simple, stupid." You *can* get by with the basics (see sidebar above).

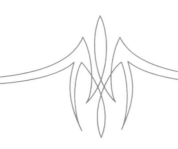

My Colorado/California traveling box expanded after my last trip to the Bakersfield Hot Rod Reunion. I picked up this plastic tackle box at a local shop in Fruita, Colorado, for under $10 while having a flat tire repaired. In it I carry basic paint colors from which you can mix most colors, reducer, a roll of tracing paper, a quart of wax and grease remover, isopropyl alcohol, a clipboard palette with my cup holders, paper cups, a few rolls of tape, and Stabilo pencils. I've lost count of how many cars I've worked on from this simple box.

This is a new addition to my kit, custom-made by my friend, Jake Yenny. It's a small collapsible tripod with a quick-release palette that fits inside my traveling box. When you take to the road you will find creative ways to consolidate and simplify the things you need.

I made my folding "show" table to fold flat so it only takes up about 1 1/2 inches of space and slides neatly into the bed of my truck. It has a paper-towel holder, holes for cups and airbrushes, a garbage bag, a palette, and the kitchen sink.

With a little PVC pipe, you can make a collapsible table that comes apart quickly.

This antique paint box/bench seat is a good example of using a little creativity to make the most out of a simple box.

Here is the same antique combo box used as a table for another paint kit.

CHAPTER 4
SURFACE PREPARATION

In life we know that nothing worthwhile can be created on a bad foundation. The same principle applies to lettering and pinstriping vehicles. If the surface of a vehicle is not clean and free from all contaminants such as wax, grease, lubricants, fingerprints, silicones, dirt, and the like, the paint you use will not adhere properly. You may invest hours creating a beautiful work of art only to have it peel off—and your reputation with it. Take the necessary steps in preparing surfaces so you will never have to endure the humiliation of redoing all your hard work at your own expense.

The car-care business is continually coming up with new "miracle paint-protection systems" to sell to the automotive enthusiast who wants a clean and shiny vehicle. These products contain ingredients such as Teflon, polymer, acrylic, exotic oils, and wax. There is no end to the combinations of elements that manufacturers will use in their quest to outshine the competition. As a professional striper you must stay informed of all the new products in this ever-changing market and arm yourself with the correct equipment to battle the removal of these invisible, slippery contaminants.

Using these surface-preparation products reduces the possibilities of surface contamination.

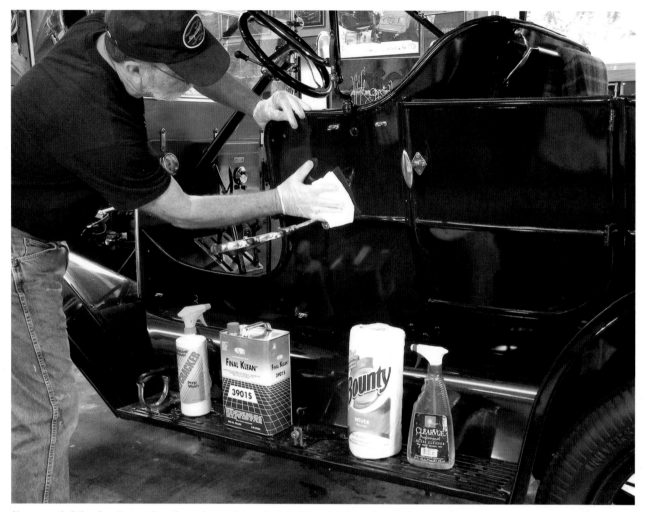

Always read all the directions and cautions of any paint products before using them. Use vinyl examination gloves to protect your skin and prevent toxic chemicals from entering your blood stream.

Preparing the surface of the vehicle with a quality wax and grease remover is key to an excellent job. Be sure to read the safety sheets on all paint-related products *before* testing anything on a customer's vehicle and then carefully adhere to those instructions.

Static electricity can build up while wiping the surfaces of fiberglass or plastic car and motorcycle parts. The resulting charged surface can actually pull the paint out of the brush before the brush makes contact with the surface. Although the resulting random patterns made by the paint are interesting, they are practically impossible to duplicate or use in a design. To eliminate a static charge, slowly wipe the surface with denatured alcohol or an anti–static cling dryer sheet. Your

paint supplier may also carry products specifically made for eliminating static electricity from plastic bumpers. I have had success eliminating static charge by spraying water on the underside of these surfaces before I begin to stripe them.

The first time I was confronted with this electrifying problem I had to stripe a Corvette that was late getting to the car show, as usual. As I started to stripe, the paint was sucked out of the brush before the tip touched the car. The result was a crazy lightning effect of paint squiggles—not a stripe. I proceeded to tape grounding wires all over the car and even poured water on the floor in an attempt to eliminate the problem. With all the wires hanging off it, the car looked like something from a Frankenstein movie, but it worked.

DuPont Final Klean 3901S is a fast-drying, fairly aggressive surface cleaner that removes most tough oil-based contaminants such as tar and lubricants. My trick is to partially loosen the cap, allowing the contents to drip out in a controllable measure onto the paper towel. This also eliminates any chance of contamination to the rest of the container.

After prepping show vehicles for many years I've come up with this three-step, 99-percent worry-free preparation system:

Step 1: Wipe DuPont Final Klean 3901S over the entire surface to be painted. There are many types of surface cleaners designed for different conditions. Some are more aggressive and faster- or slower-drying than others. Research paint products with your paint supplier to find those that best meet your needs.

Step 2: Repeat the process with Polycracker, an odorless, water-based cleaner made to remove polysilicones like Armor All and mold releases. Using plenty of Bounty paper towels or clean rags, carefully wipe the Polycracker off the surface until it is dry,.

Step 3: To remove any residues left behind in this process, repeat with a 50/50 mix of isopropyl alcohol and water or with denatured alcohol. I use ClearVue glass cleaner for this step; it has alcohol in it and it works fine for me.

Polycracker is an odorless water-based product that removes polysilicones (hence the name), which are the main ingredients in many of today's paint protection systems. Polycracker is an especially useful product while working at cars shows.

As a final step before painting any vehicle, I wipe the surface dry with ClearVue glass cleaner and Bounty paper towels. A 50/50 mixture of water and isopropyl alcohol will give a similar result. Denatured alcohol can also be used to remove anything that might have been left behind in the cleaning process.

To layout a rough idea of spacing for stripes, I draw guidelines with a water-soluble Stabilo pencil. I tend to use my fingers as a spacing guide. Get in the habit of wiping pencil dust from the surface with a tack rag just before you paint. It is comforting to know that all your hard work will not peel off when the customer washes their vehicle for the first time.

CHAPTER 5
LAYOUT AND DESIGN

There are numerous styles of pinstriping. In this chapter I will focus on symmetrical and asymmetrical designs.

Symmetrical pinstriping designs have exact corresponding lines on either side of a centerline or *axis*. The perfection of this symmetry is one of the most fascinating aspects of this style of pinstriping. When studied, some perfectly

Symmetry must be carefully executed no matter what the design is painted on. If a line goes astray, it is better to wipe everything off and start over than to have a bad design travel around with your name on it.

executed geometric pinstriping designs can focus the mind into an almost meditative state, like viewing Hindu yantra designs. Whether the design is simple or complex, the effect is the same.

Asymmetrical pinstriping designs, on the other hand, are random in nature. An excellent example is scrollwork. Even though this style is not symmetrical, it must still be balanced in weight to be pleasing to the viewer. Some striping designs can develop as you paint in a freeform way. This "create as you go" method allows for freedom in creativity.

PRACTICE PANEL

You're going to practice . . . right? Passion for striping is the power that makes practice an adventure, not a chore. Anything worthwhile requires practice.

A good practice panel is an aluminum sign blank available in various colors and sizes from sign supply companies. You can also try practicing on glass, plastic, bathroom wallboard, or any

I have always been fascinated by the symmetry of pinstriping designs. As a kid, I would stop and stare at the designs on deck lids in store parking lots. On this panel I employed a wood-grained background with some gold-leaf teardrops and very tight interweaving of color.

This panel by Jack Lindenberger is a good example of balance. Even though the design is not symmetrical, it is has a graceful flow and balance. Notice the subtle female figure.

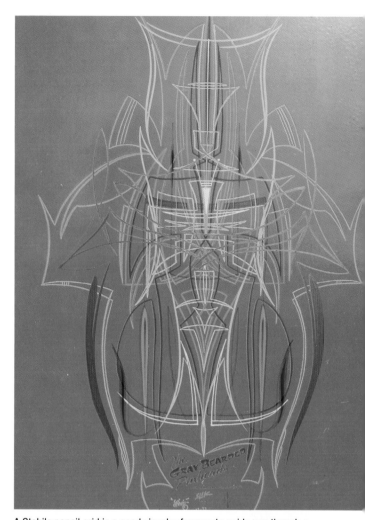

A Stabilo pencil grid is a good visual reference to guide you though a design, especially when you are working on a panel with other artists. This panel was laid out with a grid so that eight or so pinheads (affectionately known as the "Graybeards") could find a path through the maze of stripes.

other hard, glossy material. Glossy or slick surfaces can be wiped off and reused again and again.

GRID LAYOUT

A grid layout can be drawn lightly onto the panel surface with a water-soluble Stabilo pencil. Stabilo pencils are available in a variety of colors, but white and blue are preferred for most striping. These pencils are wax-free, allowing you to paint directly over them without any problems. Many seasoned stripers draw grids to keep a design symmetrical. A grid layout

is very helpful when working together with other stripers on a multicolored "panel jam."

TRANSFERRING DESIGNS

When designs are very complex, some stripers sketch them on paper first, then transfer the design to the vehicle with Saral paper, a wax-free transfer paper available in a variety of colors that will be visible on any colored surface. Think of it as carbon paper for your metal surface. A piece of Saral paper is placed between *continued on page 39*

Above: Intricate designs are best sketched on paper that allows you to retain small details accurately.

Left: Designs are easily traced using a sheet of Saral paper of contrasting color. This leaves a clear, accurate image that can be painted over and wiped off after the paint dries.

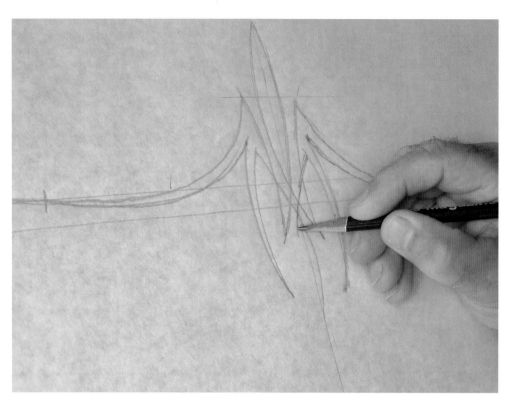

Try making a pounce-pattern layout. Draw a design on paper with an ordinary pencil, making a few horizontal and vertical guidelines to assist you in keeping your design straight and accurate. Like an old friend told me, "Work all your mistakes out on paper first."

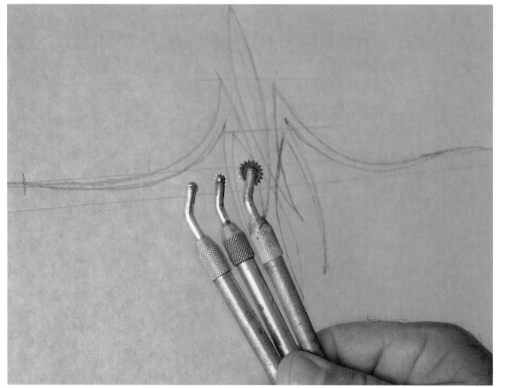

There are several sizes of patternmaking pounce wheels to choose from. These vary in size and tooth count, and can be found in most art supply stores. They are also used to make dress patterns and can be found in sewing shops.

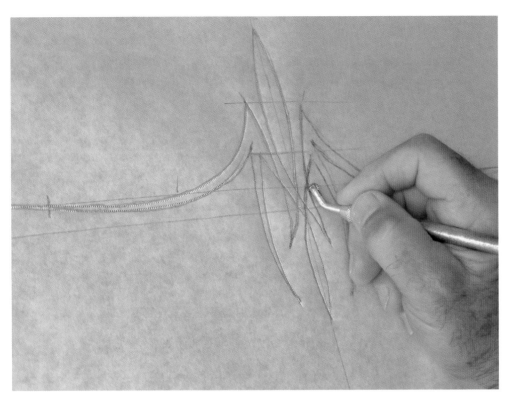

Retrace your drawing with a pounce wheel, using a little pressure on a soft surface (like cardboard) so the wheel perforates the paper. Take your time and get all the lines and details.

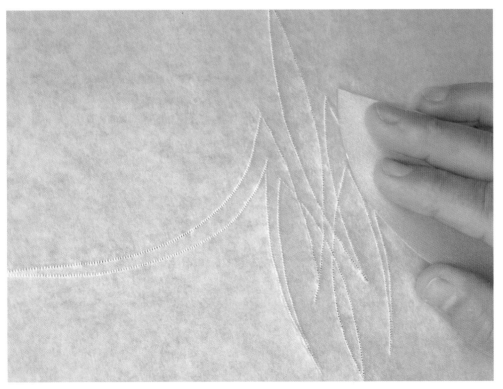

Turn the pattern over when you finish and lightly sand the perforations that the wheel has made. This will open them and allow the powder to go through the holes easily.

This photo demonstrates how you can see through the perforations after sanding the pounce pattern. Securely tape the pattern in position on the surface so it will not move when you "pounce" it.

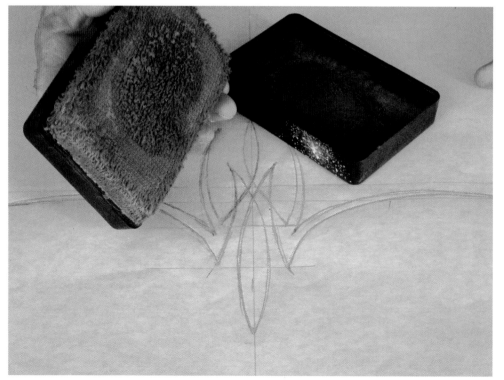

There are different kinds of pounce bags and boxes that you can find in a good art or sign supply store. I generally use an old sock that is filled with powder and tied in a knot, but this box with charcoal powder in it may be more to your liking.

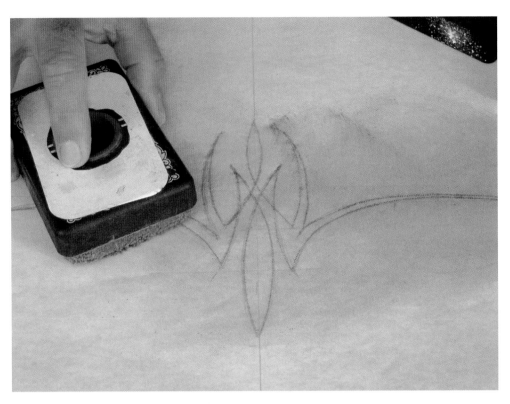

Simply rub pounce powder over the pattern, making sure you cover every area you have perforated.

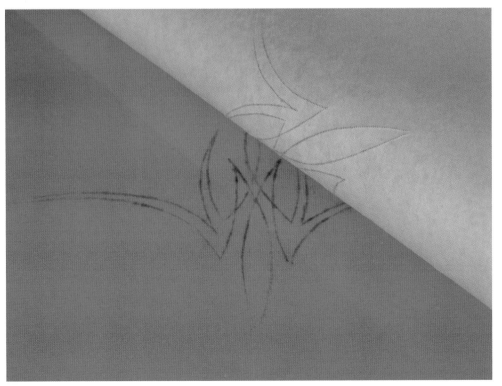

Before you remove the pattern, take a peek under it to see that all the details have been transferred. Carefully remove the pattern, lightly blow off any excess powder, and you are ready to paint.

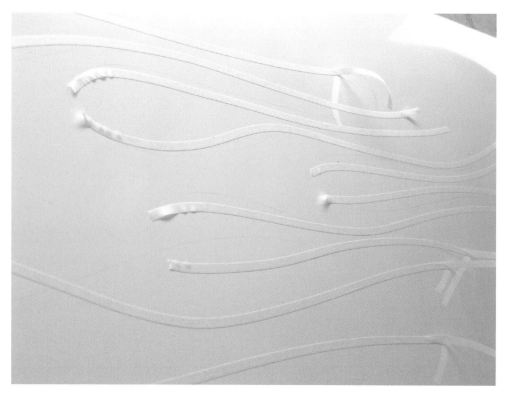

Some stripers use this tape method to lay out a flame pattern. I used 1/4-inch masking tape for this demonstration. It is fairly flexible and easy to work with.

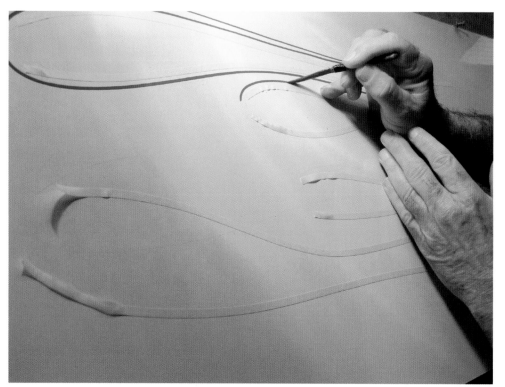

Next, follow close to the tape of your rough flame layout with the brush. Leave enough room between the flames so you can adjust the design as you stripe.

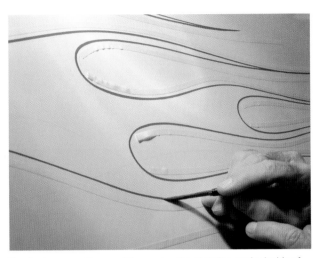

Use the tape as a finger guide, running the pinstripe on the inside of the flame shape.

Here you can see how to run the pinstripe out the open ends of the tape flame layout. The tape is only a rough guide for your finger to follow.

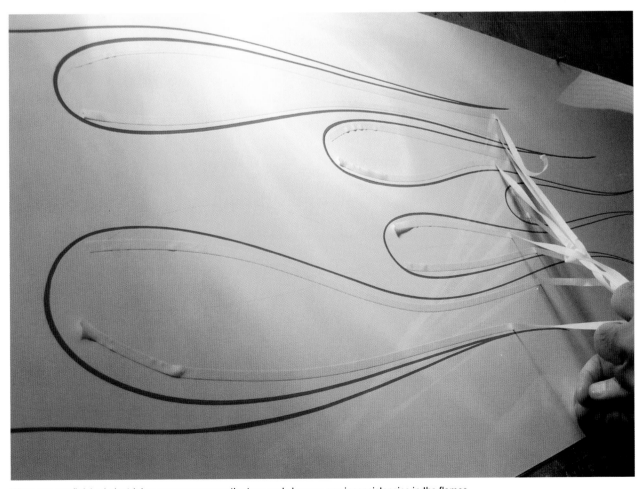

When you are finished pinstriping, you can remove the tape and clean up any inconsistencies in the flames.

Tape can be useful to find the center of a rounded or unusually shaped surface. Lightly draw a line on each side of the tape with a Stabilo pencil and you are ready to paint.

This is an example of a simple single-color design. You don't have to get carried away, especially at a car show, to create good art. Try and keep it simple.

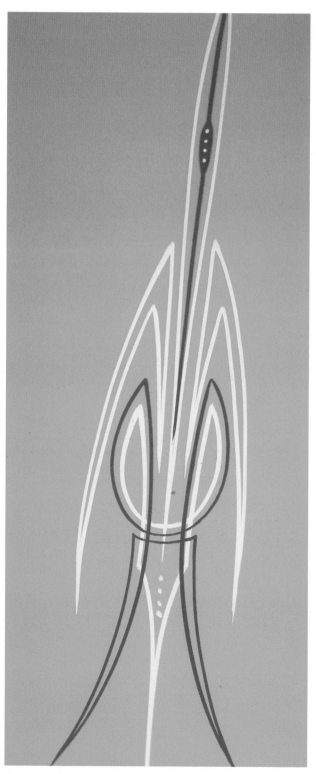

Two colors can add more interest to a design. Take the time to maintain good flow and balance throughout your design.

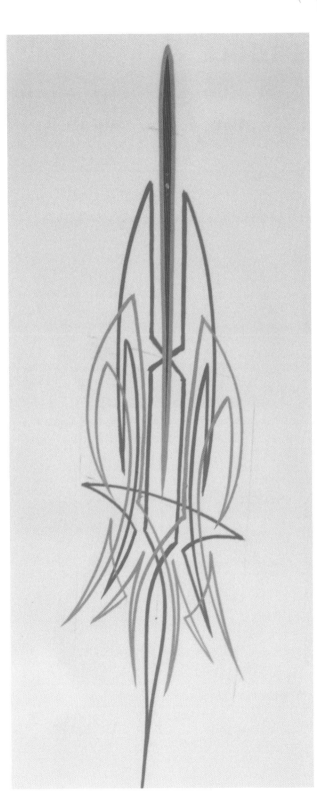

When executing a three-color image, be sure to plan ahead how you will weave the colors together in a pleasing harmony.

continued from page 30

the paper pattern and the surface, and then the pattern is retraced, transferring it to the surface. This is a good way to duplicate intricate designs without loosing any of the complexity.

POUNCE PATTERNS

Another tried-and-true method to transfer a design is to *pounce out* a pattern. Manual pounce patterns are produced by rolling a small star-shaped pounce wheel over the design. The sharp wheel perforates the paper, producing a pounce pattern. Then the pattern is flipped over and lightly sanded with fine sandpaper to open the small perforations, allowing pounce powder to pass through easily.

Another mechanism that produces the same perforated effect is an electro pounce. This machine is typically not portable; it consists of an electrified stylus that creates small intermittent electrical sparks when placed near a metal surface. The stylus burns a series of holes through the paper pattern, creating a single line of perforations. If you choose to use an electro pounce, be mindful that it can also give you a pretty exciting jolt if you are not paying attention.

After the pattern is perforated using either method, tape the pattern in position and dust colored powder over the surface of the paper pattern. The pounce powder goes through the perforations to the surface of the vehicle. Duplicating an image this way is smart when producing the same design over and over again. Good patterns can be carefully filed and reused for years.

TAPE

There are many ways that tape can be used as a guide. Most stripers use 1/4- or 1/8-inch flexible masking tape for finger or hand guides to paint lines. Others use a thin magnetic strip as a guide; it is stretched out along the body of the car when striping long straight lines. Tape can also be used as a centerline starting point for designs.

Many stripers use thin, flexible tape to layout pinstriped flames. The taped flames are laid out in an open-ended fashion. The tape then works as a guide for the brush. Using this method, you can lay out a flame design quickly with tape to see how the design will look before you pinstripe the flames. If you want to reproduce the same flames on the opposite side of the vehicle, you can do so by tracing the taped design onto tracing paper, making a pounce pattern of the design, and pouncing it on the other side. Tape can also be used to find the center of a rounded object that you are striping.

continued on page 43

USEFUL TOOLS

Tools can be found where and when you least expect them. You might be surprised what you can improvise to make life a little easier, especially when you are away from your studio. A business card can be used in any number of creative ways. I carry one in my daily business planner everywhere I go. It is marked with almost every antique-rim-striping measurement I have encountered. I just hold it to the edge of the rim and make a mark with a Stabilo and I am ready to stripe. Keep your eyes and mind open for useful and unusual stuff to help in everyday work. It will also help to keep your imagination bright.

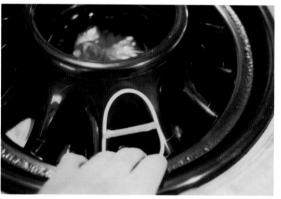 

Simple things lying about will often serve as helpful tools. I taped together the plastic core from an empty roll of tape, and it made a perfect template for the striping on this early Willys rim. I traced the template with a Stabilo then followed that with the striping brush.

A clothespin I found in my apron worked as a measuring guide for the pinstripe around the hub and the edge of the rim. I used the clothespin to create a stable distance that I followed with a Stabilo pencil before pinstriping.

Here is the reason that the clothespin was in my apron: it makes a great clamp to hold brushes in the cleanout container filled with mineral spirits.

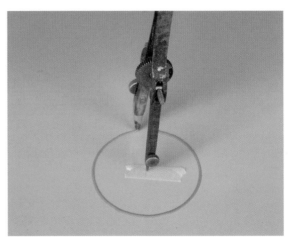

You can use a drafting compass to paint a perfect circle. On the surface to be painted, place a small piece of tape as a center for the compass tip. Use a brush to carefully load the compass with your paint mixture.

Adjust the compass to be the same width as your pinstriping and gently give it a controlled spin. You will have to experiment with the paint consistency to get the desired results.

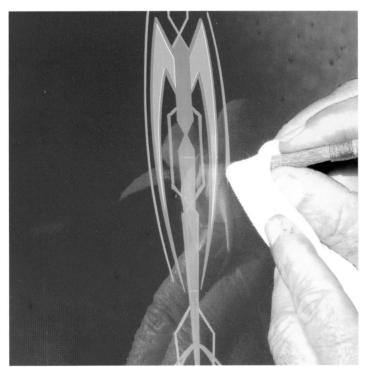

To clean up a mistake in a line or design, use a rag wrapped over the end of the brush handle. Push the handle of the brush toward the mistake and push the mistake back into the stripe. Sometimes a small amount of denatured alcohol on the rag works best to completely remove the excess paint residue from a mistake. You can also clean up a mistake with a cuticle stick and the same method. Carry the stick with you in your apron. And, by the way, you can pick up your apron at most any lumberyard for free.

USEFUL TOOLS (CONTINUED)

As I mention later in Chapter 8, you need to open the hood sides on some antique and classic cars to stripe them properly. Set the hood edge on a firm cushion. I found this piece of foam in the upholstery area of the shop.

A test panel is a good tool to help the customer choose a color. Test panels can be made from any scrap of metal that is painted the same color as the car.

continued from page 39
BALANCE

However you decide to transfer and paint your designs, keep it simple at first. It is better to paint as many simple practice pieces as possible, getting used to paletting the paint and brush.

Remember, in any great artwork, it is what is left out that makes it great. Less is more. Always maintain simplicity in creating an interesting design. That's not as easy as it sounds. Start with a single-color design, then add a second color. Try to maintain a pleasing structure and balance in your designs; they don't need to be too busy to be interesting.

Unfortunately, many vehicle graphics over the past several years are nothing but a mass of clutter. A well-known automotive artist friend of mine, Don Boeke, named this style "scrambled graphics." "It looks as if some painters cleaned out their paint cabinets on the cars," Don tells me. Personally, I'm glad that fad is gone for the most part and has given way to clean, simple, and tasteful graphic designs.

Design clutter is not a modern phenomenon; it has reared its ugly head throughout the centuries. M. C. Hillick addressed this issue over 100 years ago in his book, *Practical Carriage and Wagon Painting*. "A riotous jumble of colors thrown into a fine line corner piece or scroll is an abominable exhibition of bad taste," he wrote. "A glaring badge of cheapness is the ornament constructed from an inharmonious selection of colors." Don't get me wrong—I've gone over the edge more than once. But my best and most admired work is that of creative simplicity and taste.

You may recognize some of the strokes we will practice . . . .you are going to practice, aren't you?

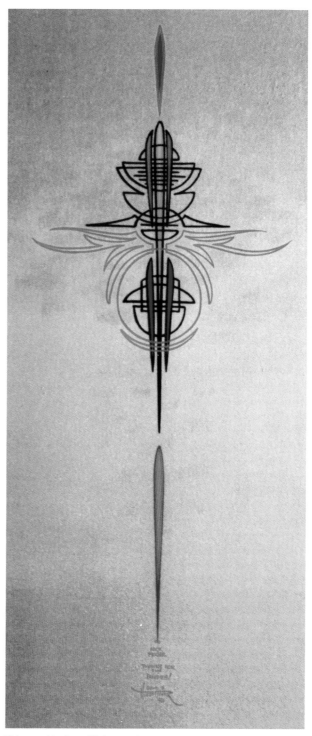

This panel by Dave Hightower is a great example of excellent use of color and thinking through a design. See how clean this design is? Even though it is complex and multicolored, it still has a simple flow that is pleasing to the eye.

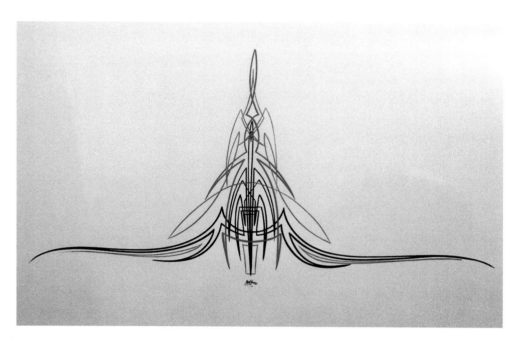

With a four-color design, you run the risk of getting lost in the maze if you don't plan ahead. Start with the most contrasting color, followed by a middle tone and so on, ending with the least contrasting color.

The old Speedball lettering book inspires this striping style by Penttila. Most of us "Graybeards" grew up with the Speedball book, which contained Italian engraving fonts. There are many variations of this classic style around today.

Faces and other animated characters are sometimes incorporated into old-school striping designs.

Typical old-school striping is often red and white, but I prefer to use what I call "dirty whitewall" and "deep, muddy red" on a flat-black primer or suede background.

A quick two-color design is sometimes all that is needed on a simple, nostalgic hot rod. But remember these two things: 1) even simple designs must be thought out in advance, and 2) you must train yourself to know when to stop and wash out the brush.

This '32 coupe has all the correct old-school stuff: two-tone rolled and pleated interior, Buick nailhead with old speed equipment for power, and Buick drums for stopping. Matching the two-color striping to the interior was a no-brainer.

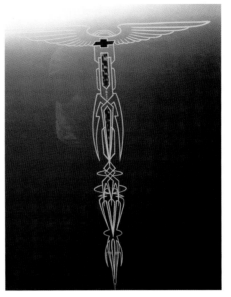

Sometimes you can get carried away if the vehicle calls for it. This is a case of a vehicle being left in my shop too long.

This complex Art Deco–style striping, which I painted on the rear of a beautiful '47 Olds sedan delivery, adds to its overall look. Notice how the gold leaf, the Chevy emblem, and the grille motif are all integrated into the design.

This highly modified two-door wagon needed a modern approach to set off the horizontal lines of the tailgate.

CHAPTER 6
BRUSH TECHNIQUE

TRIMMING THE BRUSH

To trim or not to trim, that *is* the question. In the past some stripers cut the *belly* from the striping sword so the brush could paint tight turns or scrolls without the shorter belly hairs kicking out on the turns. But today you can find any number of brushes specifically designed to handle the smallest turns and scrolls that your imagination can conceive. With all the different brush styles that are available today, I no longer see the need to trim or restyle an already perfectly designed brush.

Some new brushes are treated with a substance that keeps the hairs straight, and in some cases stiff, during shipping. This *size* can be washed out with a little warm water; I use water and a drop of hair conditioner to straighten the hairs. When you look closely at the new brush, you may see a few wild hairs sticking out of the side or past the tip. These can be combed into submission with a little warm water and a small parts-cleaning brush or an acid brush.

The next step with a new brush is to dip it into quality brush oil. Using my fingers, I completely work neat's-foot oil or lemon oil into the hair of the brush, especially the *heel*, directly near the *ferrule* (the band that holds the bristles to the handle). Once oiled, form the brush back to its natural pointed shape. Should you find a few disruptive hairs that need to be removed, carefully cut them or pull them out with tweezers to properly shape the brush. Typically, a new brush has one or two hairs that protrude past all the other hairs at the tip. If these are left untrimmed, the brush will not make good beginnings or endings to your stripes. A slightly blunt or squared-off tip can be achieved by trimming with caution, removing only the longer hairs from the tip. If too much of the tip is trimmed, it will be too blunt for fine work and relegated to use on garbage-truck striping.

An acid brush can be used to comb out most of the wild hairs that make a brush hard to manage. You need to road-test some brushes for awhile until they are broken in.

Oiling the brush before you get paint on it helps keep the heel or ferrule free from paint buildup. If paint dries in the ferrule, the hair will become brittle and fall out prematurely.

After oiling the brush you may still find some wild hairs that need to be trimmed (I fondly call them Willie Nelson hairs). Take care when removing these hairs. Sometimes I beat up a new brush striping big trucks until they loosen up enough to conform to finer detail work.

PALETTING THE BRUSH

Before we start painting, all the oil needs to be completely washed out of the brush with mineral spirits. Using a double cup holder, add a small amount of paint to the cup on the right; in the left, add some reducer that corresponds to the present weather conditions. Choosing the reducer to fit the weather makes a big difference in the flow of the paint. First, dip the tip of the brush into the reducer, then into the paint and work them both into the brush by *paletting* the brush, dragging it back and forth on the palette (a clipboard with an old magazine make for a fine pinstriping palette). If you feel the paint is too thick, dip the tip of the brush into the reducer only; if the paint feels too loose, dip the brush into the paint only and bring it back to the palette again.

Although some new brushes are just perfect and ready to go, most need a bit of grooming to make them paint perfectly. The Mack Series 10 brushes are still made by hand, as they have been since the 1890s. These beauties may vary slightly from brush to brush. Only a few hairs should be cut to create a blunt point that will make all the difference. Begin to pay close attention to pinstriping at car shows, notice the different ways stripers end their lines.

Above: Paletting the brush is a very important process to get the paint to correct consistency so it will flow smoothly. Dip the brush first into the reducer, then into the paint cup. Mix and palette the brush until you reach a smooth drag. Its like love—you'll know it, when you find it.

Left: Loading a brush with the correct mixture of reduced paint depends on many factors that you will learn from the most reliable teaching combo: trial and error. This process must not be taken lightly. Practice and experimentation are paramount in understanding the nature of the paint.

Recently I saw a photo in a book, *Hot Rods of the '50s* by Andy Southard, that shows Von Dutch striping. I noticed that I stripe with the same two-handed, overhand method that he used. I guess if he did it that way, so can I. Don't worry about the critics— just grab the brush and paint!

It will take time to learn this process and proper paint consistency. If the paint is too thick, it will not flow smoothly— it will drag and skip. Thinning or reducing the paint too much will make it too watery or runny and render the brush uncontrollable. The correct paint-to-reducer ratio is found when the brush glides smoothly and does not stick to or grab the palette as you drag it back and forth, working the paint into the brush. *Drag, flow, skip,* and *bleed* are some terms we use to describe paint consistency. Reaching the proper paint consistency is best learned by trial and error. You will learn more about the character of the paint by overthinning and underthinning it than I can explain in words. If you encounter brush-handling problems, chances are the paint consistency is incorrect.

LOADING THE BRUSH

The paleting process is how the brush becomes filled or *loaded* with paint. When you paint long lines, a full load of a thinner mixture is required to stripe the entire distance at a faster rate of speed. When you paint designs, less paint and a slightly thicker mixture is required for shorter lines, as these are painted at a slower rate of speed. In both cases the line consistency is controlled by the paint consistency.

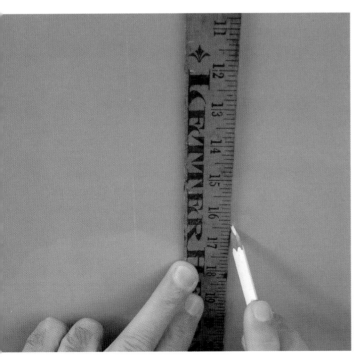

For the exercises in this chapter, lightly draw a center guideline with a Stabilo pencil. Use a color that is not too bright or contrasting. You need it only for a reference point.

BRUSH GRIP

Gently grip the brush between your thumb and forefinger as you would a pencil. Steady your hand with your pinky or other fingers. You can also use your other hand to steady the brush hand. Techniques for steadying the striping hand vary widely among stripers. Some use the remaining fingers of the brush hand flat on the surface to steady their hand. Experiment with all the fingers not holding the brush, and you will find the most comfortable way for *you* to steady your hand. I've tried them all, but whichever method you feel comfortable with is the right one. I use a two-handed method similar to the one Von Dutch used.

Know-it-all pinstripers have told me over my entire career that I stripe backward, the "wrong" way or "upside down." Now I just smile as I think of all the hot rods and classic cars I've worked on over the years that have won first-place honors in shows, such as those I striped for the Pebble Beach Concours. So don't worry about how you finally decide to grip the brush—you're in good company. If your results are good and you feel comfortable, it doesn't matter if you stand on your head.

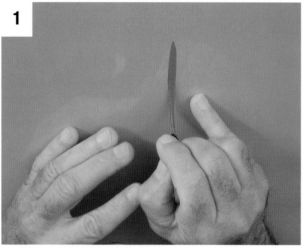

1: With your paint mixed to a smooth consistency, load your brush. Hold the brush in a comfortable **grip** at the top of your panel and push the brush down and forward as far as it will go without yet moving it toward you. Notice how wide a blob your brush can make.

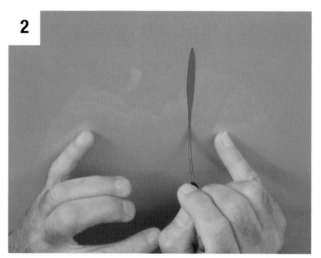

2: With your hands at the top of the panel, tilt your hands forward and down to make a thick blob. Pull slowly toward you, lifting up and back to a thin line. As you go through these exercises, remember to keep paletting paint into your brush to maintain the same workable consistency.

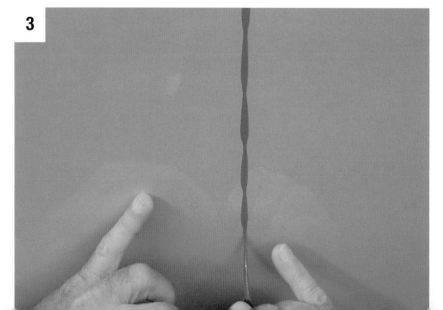

3: Repeat this up-and-down motion as you pull the brush down the panel. Just play with the brush and discover what it can do—you will wipe this panel clean many times. Try another ribbon of thick and thin shapes, gaining control of the brush to make smooth transitions from thick to thin.

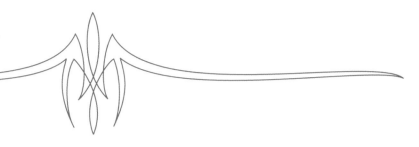

BRUSH PRESSURE

Your hands and body are becoming a "paint machine." Soon you will find you can draw a straight line without a ruler. To paint well, you need to be agile, as there is a considerable amount of body movement involved when your hand or hands are locked on the brush grip.

By tilting your hands forward and down toward the surface, you add more down pressure to the brush, which produces a wider line. Tilting the hands backward and up lifts the brush and produces a thinner line.

With your hands at the top of your practice panel, tilt your hands forward and down to make a thick blob. Pull the brush slowly toward you, lifting it up and back to thin the line, and then tilting it back down again. Repeat this up-and-down motion as you pull the brush down the panel. Discover what the brush can do—you will wipe your practice panel clean many times.

BRUSH SPEED

The size of a brush is designed to produce a certain line thickness that changes slightly as you adjust the pressure up and down.

Now, with your practice panel lying flat on a table in front of you, place your hands at the top of the panel, set your brush grip, at a heavy-line pressure, and slowly pull

1: You should now know what widths your brush is capable of from the previous page. Starting with a clean palette page, dip into reducer and paint, and palette again to the proper consistency. With your hands at the top of the panel, adjust your **pressure** to a heavy line and slowly pull your hands towards you at a steady **speed**, all the way to the bottom of the panel.

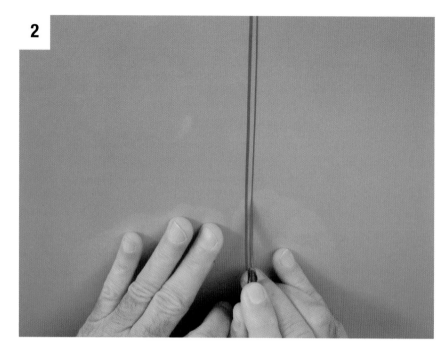

2: Between strokes, palette your brush until you are ready to restart. With your hands at the top of the panel, begin again close to the heavy line. Adjust your pressure to a thin line and slowly pull your hands toward you at a steady speed, all the way to the bottom of the panel.

your hands toward you, moving your body backward as you go. Note how much your body needs to move to keep your hands steady and locked on the brush grip.

Next, start at the top and move slowly toward you in the same manner but with a thin-line pressure. Now, practice painting thick and thin lines from left to right on the whole panel until you find the stripe thickness which that particular brush will produce. Next, practice pulling consistent lines of the same thickness from left to right, about an inch apart over the whole panel. You didn't know there would be homework did you?

Although the straight line is the most basic pinstriping design element, it is not the easiest to master. Pressure, speed, and practice are the keys to excellence.

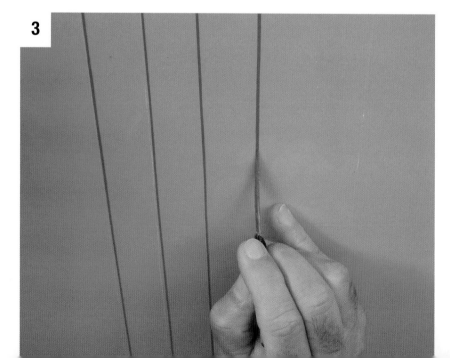

3: Repeat a series of lines of a thickness that you find you are most comfortable with. If you are experiencing any inconsistency in line quality, go back to your palette to work out the paint and brush until it feels smooth with a little drag.

BRUSH ANGLE

To make anything other than straight lines you need to add the final element. Hold the brush loosely, not heavy-handed, so you can manipulate it, and then fine-tune this movement. Holding the brush gently, twirl it slightly to the left (counterclockwise) and right (clockwise) between your fingertips. This movement steers the brush left and right as if you were cutting a path with a knife. Now that your "paint machine" is locked to the consistent line-quality position, smoothly move it toward you. With just a slight twirling motion you can direct the brush left and right as you go. Practice pulling consistent lines of the same thickness and speed, but twisting from left to right and from right to left as if the brush was skiing down a mountainside.

1: The **brush angle** is controlled with a slight twist of the fingers from right to left. While your hands and arms move in a machine-like way, you must hold the brush gently so it can be directed with your fingers.

2: Incorporate the same **brush pressure** and steady **brush speed** that you used in the first two exercises. Start at the top of the panel with a left angle to the brush. Slowly twist the brush to the right and back again to the left on down the panel.

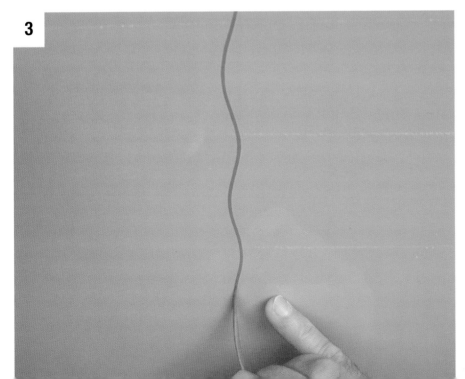

3: Repeat these left and right turns as if the brush were a knife cutting through cardboard. The brush tip is the same shape as a knife, only fluid. If you find your brush skipping out on the turns, change your angle, pressure speed, or paint consistancy.

BASIC STROKES

Before we get into the basic strokes, remember this rule: if you are right-handed it is best to work from left to right. This way, when you get to the right side you will be able to see and mirror the strokes you painted on the left. Since I am right-handed, I will describe these strokes from a right-hander's perspective. Obviously, if you are left-handed simply apply the inverse.

Teardrop Stroke

This stroke is a stylized, inverted teardrop shape popularized by Tommy "The Greek" Hrones. This stroke can be executed in two ways.

The first is to make a solid teardrop. Start at the top with the brush pressed down. Begin with a thick top portion and decrease the brush pressure as you move your hands toward you.

The second way is to paint an outline teardrop. Start at the top with your "paint machine" locked in the consistent line-quality position. Smoothly move toward you and with a slight counterclockwise twirling motion, direct the brush left and slowly back to the center. Repeat this procedure on the other half of the teardrop, but with a slight clockwise twirling motion, slowly directing the brush right and back to the center, intersecting the line on the left.

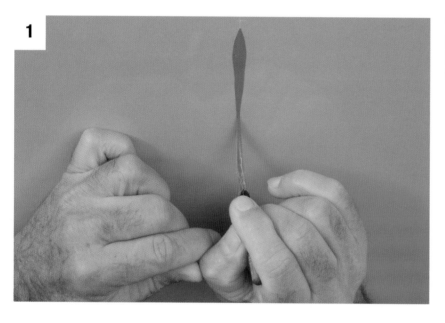

1: This inverted, stylized **teardrop** is produced with the technique you learned in the pressure exercise. The only difference is that you paint a single thick-to-thin teardrop.

2: The teardrop stroke can be executed in an outline form by incorporating the strokes you learned in the angle exercise. Start at the center and slowly turn the brush to the left then back to the center, gently lifting as you stop moving.

BRUSH TECHNIQUE

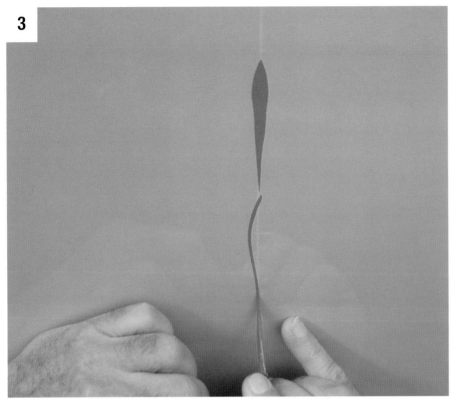

3: As you reach the end of the teardrop, gently and steadily lift the brush up off the panel in a steady motion while pulling it toward you. The teardrop shape can be elongated, compressed, or turned any way you wish to fit any design.

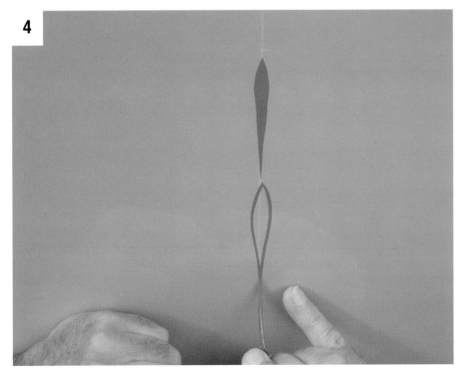

4: Repeat this same stroke but start by angling the brush to the right and move back to the center. Practice different combinations of widths and lengths of this teardrop shape.

Lazy-S Stroke

In the 1800s, ornamenters and carriage stripers referred to this stroke as the "scroller's line of beauty." It employs both the left and right turns you practiced in the "Brush Angle" section. Place the brush lightly just right of center. With a slight left angle, slowly pull down toward you. Turn the brush back toward the center, and when you reach the center turn the brush back to the left.

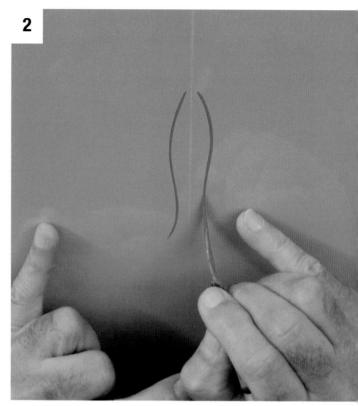

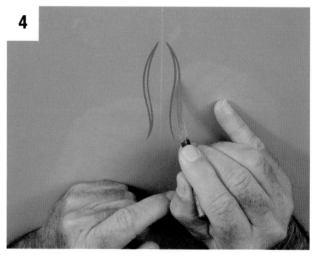

1: The **lazy-S stroke** is also produced with the techniques you learned in the angle exercise. But unlike the teardrop, which ends in the center, this stroke turns back away from the center. For a clean finish, gently lift your brush as you stop moving.

2: The right side is created the same way as the left. For a right-hander, doing the strokes on the left side of the design first allows good visibility for mirroring those left-hand strokes when striping on the right side.

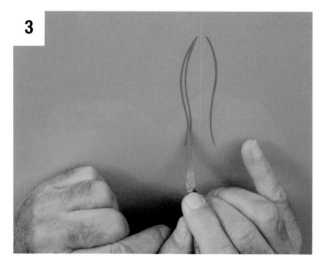

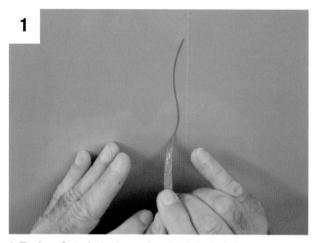

3: Any of these strokes can easily be doubled to add interest. Start at the same beginning point, separate, and return to the same ending point.

4: You can see something taking shape when you add a double stroke to any of these shapes. This technique can be useful in helping a design when you begin painting on a vehicle.

Crossover Stroke

The crossover opens up a vast territory for design possibilities. This stroke is executed in the same manner as the outlined teardrop, but instead of ending at the center you cross over to the other side of the design. This elementary stroke is essential in designs that consist of one continuous line. Place the brush at center. With a slight left angle, slowly pull down toward you. Turn the brush back toward the center and past the center point of your choice.

1: Execute the **crossover** stroke exactly as you did the outlined teardrop, but instead of ending at the center, cross over to a predetermined ending point, slowly lift up, and stop to form a blunt point.

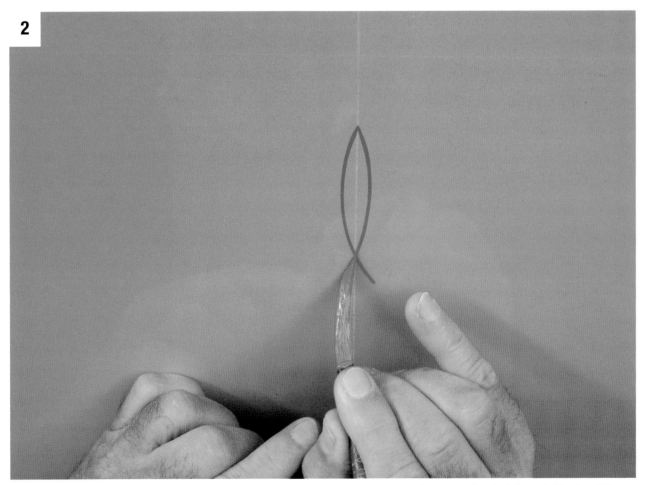

2: Mirror the first crossover with the right side and slowly lift up and stop to form a blunt point. Remember: if you're left-handed, begin painting your designs on the right side. That way, your hand won't be obscuring the already-painted side that you're trying to mirror. Also, be conscious of your peripheral vision as you paint. This will become more important as we enter the design phase.

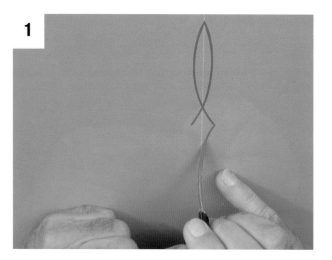

1

Ending a Stroke

There are two ways to end a stripe. For a blunt or squared-off ending, slowly lift and stop at the same time. To end a stripe with a sharp point, lift the brush off the surface as you continue to pull the brush. These two endings give you options for direction changes.

Without the passion to master these four basic strokes, your practice will feel more like work instead of fun.

1: There are two ways to **end a stroke**. A blunt-pointed ending is created by slowly lifting the brush up and stopping at the same time. A sharp-pointed ending is created by slowly lifting the brush up before you stop moving.

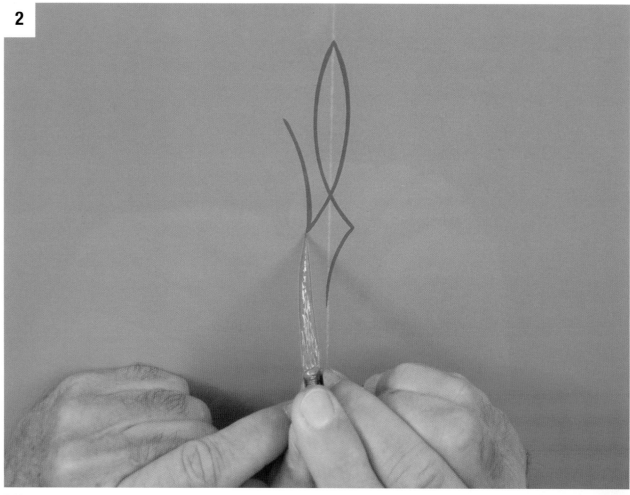

2

2: Here you can see the different types of line endings. The line ending is a small detail in the vast scheme of things, but keep learning to pay attention to all the small details and they will add up to better striping jobs. From these different ending points you can go off in all directions easily.

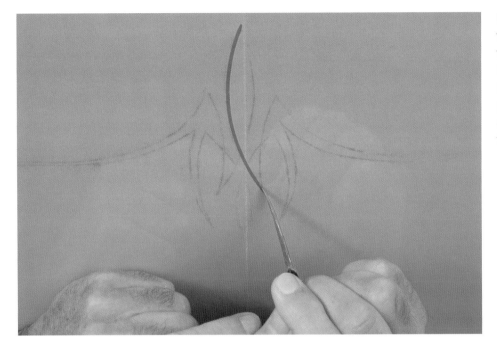

I start most of my designs without any plan, but I typically work out from the center. For this demonstration we will use the pounce pattern from the previous chapter. Let's start with a simple crossover stroke and go from there.

BASIC DESIGNS

Most pinstriping designs start at a center point and build out using these four basic strokes. A simple teardrop is a good foundation from which to build. Begin practicing single-color designs until you get comfortable with the brush and paint. I know you want to rush ahead, but go slow at first and learn to build a solid foundation of these basics strokes. Study pinstriping designs to see how they are constructed.

Draw some designs in a sketchpad; you may want to make patterns from existing designs as well. Don't be discouraged if you have trouble getting the hang of the brush right away—practice is the key to success. I once suggested to a few beginners that they should blow up their televisions and devote a few hours every evening to learning how to pinstripe. Now they are doing fantastic work. If you have ever learned

continued on page 65

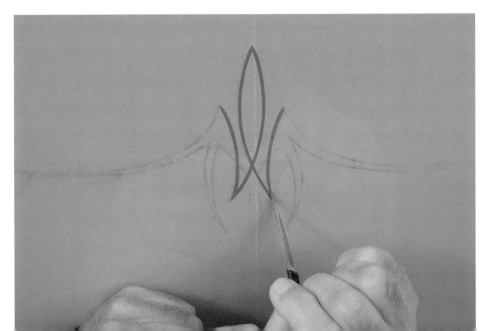

Begin with a blunt point and slowly pull the brush down to a pointed ending at the bottom of the design.

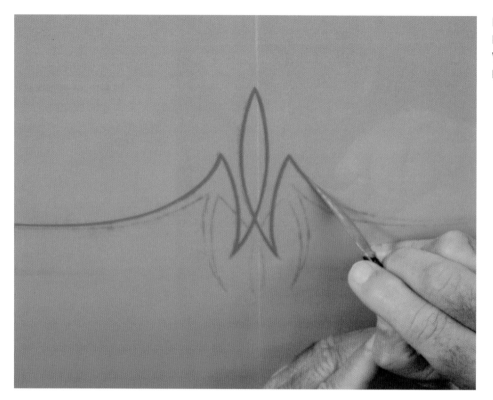

Here, I'm finishing a lazy-S stroke horizontally instead of vertically. While the strokes are the same, the hand position is changed slightly.

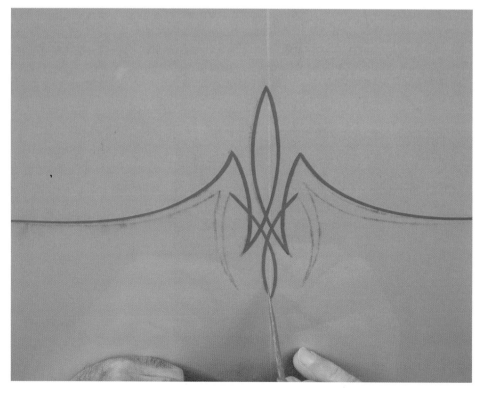

Next, I finish an inverted crossover stroke. Notice how simple it is to create a design out of these basic strokes when you use them in different ways.

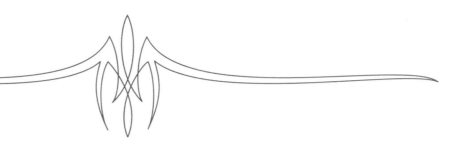

Here is a short half of a lazy-S with a pointed end that finishes the basic construction of the design. Now I think to myself, "How can I embellish this simple design?"

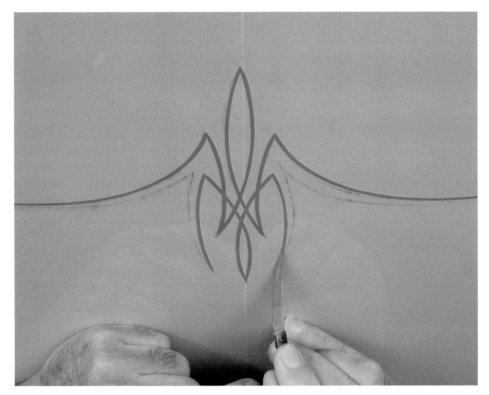

When you create a pinstriping design, try not to leave any loose ends open. I call them "Delaware disconnects," named after the style of a striper from that state. The loose ends just don't look finished to me, so why not double them up?

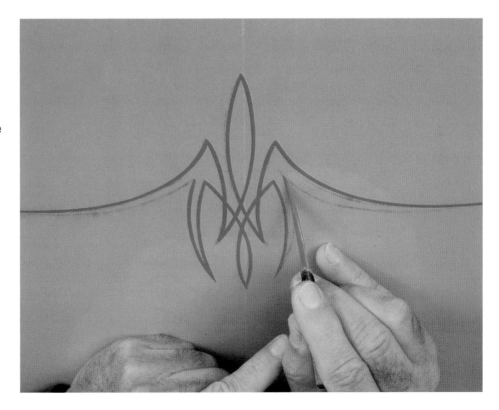

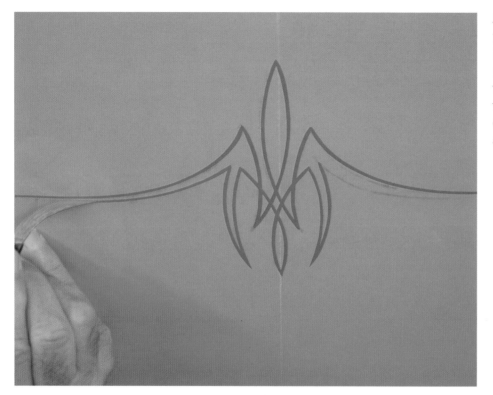

A design looks much better when you make connects rather than leave disconnects. Take a little more time laying out your designs to give it an interesting and finished look. Notice how you are developing your peripheral vision as you work a design out.

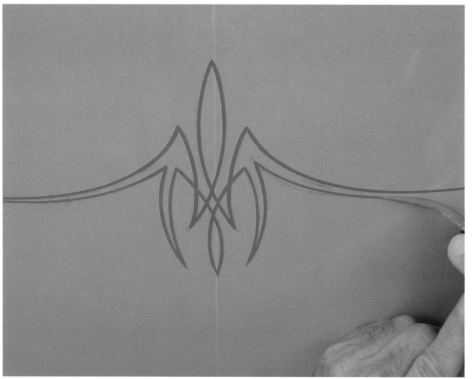

Practice this simple design with these basic strokes a few times to get used to them. Try building your own design using this as a base. Look closer at other people's striping to see if you can identify the basic strokes or variations of what you are learning. Now, turn off the idiot box and go to the garage and PRACTICE!

continued from page 61

to play a musical instrument, you know how awkward it felt at first. Pinstriping is no different. So enjoy this discovery process, just get the brush, and have fun!

BRUSH-CLEANING AND STORAGE

When you are finished striping, your brush should be rinsed thoroughly in mineral spirits. Be sure to pay special attention to the heel of the brush, directly near the *ferrule* (the band that holds the bristles to the handle), to make sure no paint is left behind. I use a clothespin to hang the brush in a jar of mineral spirits that will draw all the paint completely out of the brush in a short time.

When you are satisfied that the brush is clean, dip it into brush oil and work the oil into the hair well. Then coax the brush back into its original shape with your fingers. Store the brush flat in your brush box or in a flat metal tray.

When your brush is clean, dip it into brush oil and work the oil into the hair well. Coax the brush back into its original natural shape with your fingers and store it flat in your brush box or in a flat metal tray.

CHAPTER 7
THE STRAIGHT AND NARROW

Straight-line pinstriping is the most challenging style to master. The long, unforgiving line will show any deviations in thickness or wobble. Practice cannot be overemphasized in becoming a first-rate, straight-line specialist. Apprenticing with a professional is the best way for a beginner to grasp the subtle points of this fine craft. Of course, it helps if you are fortunate enough to find a very patient teacher as well.

Cars and pinstriping have always been synonymous . . . you know, like a horse and carriage. Line widths on carriages and antique cars were mostly pin lines that gave a delicate look and character to the vehicle. As car manufacturers changed designs from belt-molding construction to larger, flat body panels, pinstriping was used to accent these shapeless panels. As the cars grew in size, the stripes grew wider also. A pinstripe or two placed in the right spot help a car look lower and longer. As car shapes continue to change with new construction techniques, so will pinstriping applications.

We talked a little about the brush grip previously. Most straight-line or dealer stripers hold the brush in a similar manner. Most use a single-handed grip with the remaining fingers free to steady the hand. This grip is the easiest and

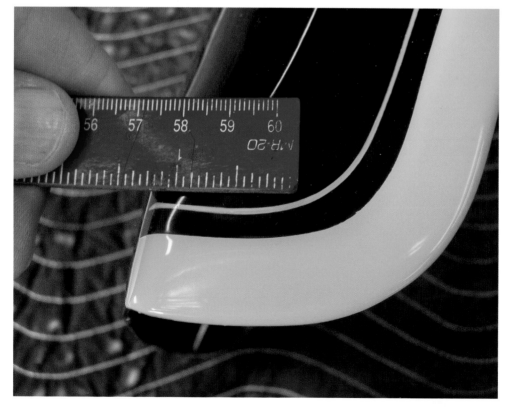

Pinstriping should be just that: a pinline, not a thick, spaghetti-like line that ruins the appearance of a beautiful restoration. Imagine what this high-contrast color combination would look like if this line were thicker. The thin line blends the color transition, making it appear softer.

This '32 coupe resto rod is striped thinner than the originals were to give it a fine, elegant look. This stripe would have to be about 1/8 inch thick for an original restoration.

that you start doing the most of determines the style of grip you develop. For instance, if you start striping designs mostly on hot rods and customs with a raised belt molding like I did, you may find the two-handed method works best. This allows you to avoid obstacles and use tight turns to adjust to the curving belts that run around the body. Stripes painted on shorter sections do not require you to load the brush too heavily. Stripes that run on the top and bottom edges of belt moldings, however, demand a twist of the wrist. Dealership stripers reading this, I'm sure, are pulling their hair out about now. I have heard some seasoned stripers swear that the single-handed method is the only way to do straight-line work. I don't think Dutch or the dapper guy in a hat and tie pinstriping on the Ford assembly line back in 1932 were doing it wrong!

With that said, I'll tell you that when my daily schedule was full of dealer work, my fingers were hurting from the grip I had developed for other types of striping. I recommend that if you choose to specialize in straight-line dealer work, you study the finer points of a few of my friends' work and their grip styles. This will give you options to try out while learning some specialized tricks of straight-line striping.

fastest one to learn. I would also say that it is the grip of choice if you plan on doing a lot of straight-line work.

But like I have said, some of us just got the brush and held it the way that felt most comfortable. The type of work

Straight lines on antique cars are typically shorter in length, with turns to compensate for the obstacles that there are to contend with. A modern car, unlike an antique, has straight, flat panels with nothing to guide your hand or eye.

MISALIGNED PANELS

Misaligned hoods can be a problem if you stripe using the belt molding as a finger guide. I come across this quite often at shows. Some hoods, like this one, can be way off the mark.

To solve this dilemma, I run a 1/8-inch piece of masking tape along the center of the belt molding to equalize the alignment trouble between the doors and hood. Paint the top and bottom stripes close to the tape and you will never notice that the hood is out of alignment.

Note the straight-line pinstriper's formal hat and smock in this photo of the 1932 Ford assembly line. *Courtesy Robert Genat collection*

I had an opportunity to talk with master straight-line pinstripers Clay White and Russ Mowry at my studio. Together, we were road-testing some experimental striping brushes that Chris Fast of the Mack Brush Company dropped by. Chris probably got more information than he bargained for on that visit. I believe the best way to create a brush for pinstripers is to have experienced stripers test them out first. We all had different opinions on the brushes and we all found a different brush to suit the way we stripe. This is why there are so many brush styles to choose from. I have tried some new brushes and found them impossible to handle

properly; other stripers can use the same brushes and praise them for the way they perform.

Working together with other pinstripers is a rare and wonderful experience, you can learn more in five minutes than you could in years on your own. The "pinhead" movement that started in the 1990s has fostered this "brotherhood of the brush." I have a copy of the original *Pinhead Fellow Pages* with all the phone numbers and addresses of pinheads from all over the world. It's dog-eared and has been revised many times with new area codes and notes. It is incredibly cool to be able to call another pinhead when you have a question or problem with a project. It is equally cool to get a call from a pinhead you never met. Once, I received a call from an unknown person with a very heavy English accent, asking me if I would be willing to come "across the pond" to attend a meet and to share my knowledge of the craft. I said, "Alright . . . who is this really?" I thought it was someone goofing on me, but it wasn't. It was Jon Lesson, a third-generation sign-writer and pinhead. We have become good friends since that phone call and that meet. This kind of camaraderie did not always exist. When I was learning, no

Russ Mowry uses the three-finger, single-handed grip and a tape finger guide. He uses the tape to determine the character or bodyline. After he paints the first line, which is usually the heavier line, he removes the tape and paints the thin line.

one would give a kid any information at all. Some would even steer you in the wrong direction for fear of competition.

Sorry for the diversion, but I just did a word count and found I needed to add a lot more to comply with my publishing agreement. So let's return to our brush road-test. Russ Mowry is known for his magnificent motorcycle striping, artwork, and type styles. When he does straight lines he uses a tape guide to run his finger along. When he stripes, he concentrates on the distance between the tape and the brush tip as the paint is leaving the brush. His brush pressure varies to control the width of the line as he moves his way along the car. Less brush pressure is applied at the beginning of a stripe with a full load of paint. The pressure is increased as the

paint flow is being used up. This pressure adjustment is not a conscious effort but something you learn to feel over time.

Watching Russ stripe inspired Clay White as a kid. He has perfected the art of effortlessly pulling a flawless straight line. Damn kids. His straight lines are some of the best I have ever seen. Clay says he locks his hand to his shoulder as one unit. He uses the other hand and arm to steady his upper body, while the bottom part of his body (feet, legs, and hips) move him slowly backward. Instead of interpreting Clay's dialog, or me trying to explain how Clay works, I'll let him tell you in his own words:

Clay White: "When I stripe a car I use 1/8-inch, green Scotch Fine Line Tape as a guide. I have found that 1/4-inch

Clay White uses 1/8-inch tape as a guide, running his middle finger along it. He paints the stripe about 3/4 inch higher than the tape.

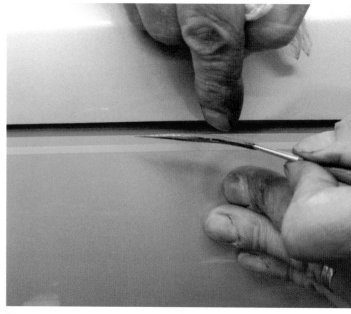

Would you like to have to redo a fender sporting this treatment by Clay?

Clay leaves the tape in place to paint both lines. Note his palette stand that is made from a camera tripod. It is adjustable, lightweight and easy to move as he works.

is too wide and my finger has too much room to 'drift' back and forth across the tape. Eighth-inch works the best for me because very little of my guide finger actually touches the paint. I hold the brush between my thumb and forefinger and use my middle finger to ride on top of the fine line. Anyone who has striped a car knows that paint varies in feel from car to car and even from panel to panel. Sometimes your finger will slide too fast if the paint is slippery or drag too much if the paint is clean, or if it's humid. Riding on top of the tape is *always* the same.

"Arm movement, body movement, brush pressure, and paint consistency are all key to great straight lines. I like to 'lock' my wrist, forearm, and upper arm as a single unit. I use my non-brush right hand (I'm left-handed) to 'feel' the top of the vehicle as a reference point. I use a crossover step to glide backward and I apply the first line approximately 1/2 inch above the guideline. I use my upper torso as a shock absorber to separate my leg movements from my arm. I focus on an area about the size of a quarter where the brush tip meets the car. I look for consistency in the weight of the line and the distance from the guideline. Then I come back and drop the next line between the first line and the guideline. To sum it up, I basically lock my arm in place, walk backward, and drag my arm along for the ride. After a lot of practice

DeWayne Connot's single-handed grip is similar to the others'. His brush, the DC Flat Liner, is designed by him and is available from the Mack Brush Company. He starts his stripe over tape that will be removed after both lines are completed to achieve a squared end.

DeWayne locks his arms and upper body into one unit from his brush hand across to his other hand, which is firmly planted on the car for balance.

DeWayne does not use the tape as a finger guide, but only as a visual guide for the first stripe. Notice how his fingers are spread out to control the brush on the side of the car.

you will find you can relax the arm a little and not be so rigid, but that won't come until way later.

"When I first started trying straight lines, a good friend of mine who was also a pinstriper gave me my first tip. He told me to imagine a point about a foot behind my elbow and drag my elbow towards it. Obviously the point has to keep moving away from you. Kind of like race dogs who chase the mechanical rabbit around the track and never actually catch up to it. It works, but the funny thing is, the friend who gave me this tip, who shall remain nameless, still cannot do straight lines.

"Another exercise is to lay down your guideline, lay down another one about a 1/2 inch above it, and try to paint

on top of the second line. It will help you know what a straight line feels like. Start by trying to keep a thin line from going off the edges of the tape line, and gradually make the line thicker and thicker until you can cover the line completely. This makes for good practice.

"My brush of choice is the old plastic-handled Grumbacher. Unfortunately they are now extinct, and I have been working with Alan Johnson, Russ Mowry, and the Mack Brush Company to come up with a good substitute.

"Paint consistency is very important. 1-Shot black straight out of the can on a warm summer day is just about perfect. I put about 1/4 inch of paint in the bottom of a 3-ounce Dixie cup. Then I add anywhere from 6 to 12 drops

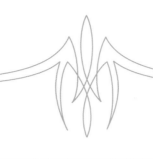

If you have to stop a stripe in the middle of a panel reload the brush and restart the stripe a few inches or more back from where you stopped. This will give you sometime to adjust the weight of the line before you get to the place where you stopped.

DeWayne points out the visual concentration zone above his brush and the first stripe. If you are a beginner, you may feel more comfortable leaving a tape guide on until you finish the striping.

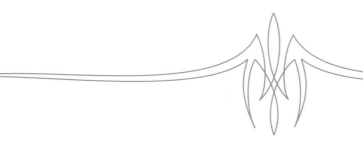

Toward the end of the line, notice how DeWayne's weight is almost all on his left foot as he rocks backward.

of thinner, depending on the color. I prefer DuPont 3864S Vari-Temp Reducer. Before I load the brush, I dip the tip of the dry brush into the thinner and work it into the brush hair with my thumb and forefinger. This helps to lubricate the brush for even paint distribution. Then dip the brush into the paint and palette it at least two dozen times to load the brush properly. The paint will only come off the brush as evenly as it is applied. I can generally stripe at least one full panel of a car, sometimes two, without reloading. Typically, every time I stop at the end of a panel, I reload the brush. It is not usually necessary to palette as many times once the brush is properly loaded."

My policy is, the larger the vehicle, the more elaborate the decoration at the line endings. Notice that Clay is left-handed and the tape guide is under the stripe. Because dealership work is nonstop, to avoid conflicts Clay schedules his work on a weekly route basis that all his customers are aware of.

This next straight line demonstration included here took place in the "Bullpen" of the USSC (United States Sign Council) Sign World trade show in Atlantic City, New Jersey. This area is sectioned off from the main hall, allowing pinheads and letterheads to paint and to share their tips and tricks with one another. There is always someone who leaves a car for us to play with, or we stripe a rental car or two. This section illustrates veteran straight-liner master DeWayne Connot's amazing skills.

DeWayne is a straight-line striping machine who has been striping for dealers and body shops in the Philadelphia area for many years. He has trained many other stripers to run a good line as well. DeWayne grips the brush in the three-finger steadying method that is common to most straight-line stripers. His brush of choice is his own Mack signature brush, the DC Flat Liner.

There are as many ways to end the lines as your imagination can conceive. This is a nice ending to a single-color double-set of stripes. Tape is laid down at a point and striped over. When the tape is removed you can cross and connect the stripes.

DeWayne stresses the importance of getting enough paint on the stripe by using a thicker paint mixture that is not over-reduced. The thicker mixture ensures better coverage that will wear longer. Plus, striping with a thicker paint can slow the process down. To maintain his speed he uses a larger brush. He holds the brush at a higher angle so only the tip touches the surface. He reloads and palettes the brush often—about every panel or so to keep the brush fully loaded. He locks his hand and shoulder and rocks backward from right to left, slowly transferring his weight from one leg to the other. His other arm is firmly planted on the car to balance and move him along at a steady pace. DeWayne uses the tape only as a visual guide and accurately maintains a constant distance between the tape and his stripe.

Doing this type of work at a fast pace while keeping your demanding customers satisfied is quite stressful, so for relaxation DeWayne enjoys painting obscure microscopic designs on panels that are almost too small to see. His unique talents as a fine artist are just an extension of the concentration it takes to do great straight-line dealership striping.

Trucks can accommodate more elaborate decoration at the line endings, as the areas are larger to work with. Let your imagination run away with you as you discover some new ideas. You can always wipe it off and start over.

CHAPTER 8
ANTIQUE AND CLASSIC CARS

GREAT CAR COLLECTORS

The owners of antique and classic cars are as unique as the cars they collect. Most are very private, some are eccentric, but typically I have found they are all successful entrepreneurs. Two constant traits among private collectors are an appreciation for the craft and an eye for detail and excellence. Results are always more important than costs.

The late Michel G. Rothschild of New Jersey, was one of my favorite collectors. Michel's entire collection consisted of early-1900s "Brass Era" cars that he drove constantly. Each machine reflected a major step in automotive technology. Michel was a real hands-on collector who did most of the machine restoration work himself. He would call me and say, "I have another one ready for the finishing touch. And this

I feel truly blessed to have been able to work in Michel Rothschild's museum. His collection was a study in automotive technology and gleaming brass. Plus, one can't help but do good work while surrounded by good lighting and music.

Working on Rothschild's collection was like working in a fancy brass shop. Michel could make almost everything he needed to restore his cars, but he never tried to paint the finishing touch. Maybe he just loved to see someone else's work included on his recreations.

time don't forget to help yourself to the food in the refrigerator." I would arrive at his beautiful home to find a note describing all the good things to eat and drink. All the doors would be unlocked, with hot coffee ready, the refrigerator fully stocked, and classical music playing throughout the house and in both floors of the shop. Michel would never make any mention of his ideas of what he wanted done to his cars, so I would access the vehicle when I arrived and paint whatever I thought was correct for that individual car. I think I striped two of his cars before we actually met each other.

One day, as I was finishing up, Michel arrived and started thrashing around in the shop above me. I went up and found him grumbling, "Why the hell did they build it this way?" He was up to his elbows in removing the transmission of his 1896 Faison. He was trying to figure out how to fabricate a new set of gears that had to include a lower ratio,

Another client's collection hosts a large variety of exotic cars. When I go to stripe a car at a collector, I study all the cars in the collection and make mental notes on the pinstriping.

When I striped this 1910 Packard, the owner and I wondered how the judges at the AACA show in Hershey would react. The happy owners won first place in their class.

It's important to photograph and study all kinds of unusual cars to see how pinstriping should be executed.

Careful study of the owner's research information reveals the correct path for striping details.

which was necessary for this beauty to climb his steep driveway. It seemed that the steering column had to be removed before he could get the transmission out. (I guess there were bad designers even at the dawn of the motorcar.) At that point I realized it was a good time to take a break and assist him. As we worked, he told me stories about his years of endurance racing with his wife at Le Mans. One story that made a profound impression on me was that they continued to race in all conditions back then, including fog at night. He told me "We would come off a right turn into a straight-away, count to 20, and blindly turn the wheel hard to the left and pray that the road would be there!"

I have been fortunate to work with notable and interesting collectors, and all of the best antique restoration shops.

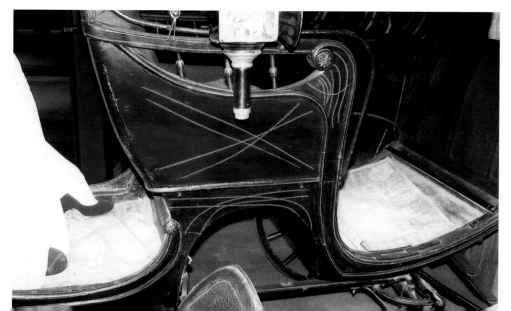

This is a fine example of what not to do. I found this in an auto museum.

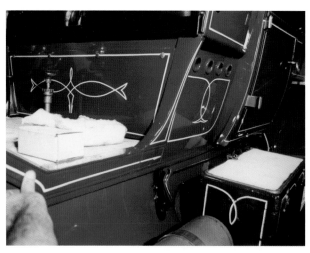

These stripes are too heavy for a car like this. They work better for a heavy-duty truck.

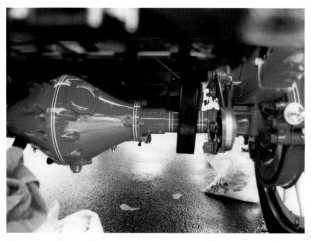

No part of this 1910 Packard was untouched by the brush, and it's just right! Even running gear received the same double-stripe treatment.

This has allowed me to work on some of the rarest vehicles known to exist in private collections nationwide—cars that consistently earn top honors at Pebble Beach and other top concours events. Collectors at this level have a common thread running throughout their personalities: it's an attitude that does not accept mediocrity in any form or the word "can't." This alone is the one concept that leads to success in any endeavor. The attitude of "quiet perfection" should be noted and adopted by any serious pinstriper planning to work in these circles.

CLASSIC AND ANTIQUE CAR STRIPING 101

Four things to contemplate before you make an appointment to stripe a priceless beauty:

1. *Be sure your business insurance is paid up; even a minor ding on one of these classics could set you back a pretty penny. Check with your insurance agent for the proper coverage for this kind of work, both in and out of your shop.*
2. *Set aside enough time to do this kind of job correctly.*
3. *Striping can be an extremely aerobic workout. It includes stretching, bending, and lying on the ground. Be sure you're limber and ready to go!*
4. *Be aware that an era-correct job includes a double stripe of the same color. Day one for stripe one, day two for stripe two (this means you do the entire job twice!).*

THE BRASS CAR ERA

Brass Era cars are really interesting and challenging to stripe. This distinction is given to the early-twentieth-century cars and stems from the obvious abundance of polished brass that was used to accessorize them. They were the first step up from horse-drawn carriages and had many of the same striping characteristics.

The first question to ask when approaching a Brass Era car is, with all the years, types, and models that exist, how do you determine where to draw the line with your pinstriping?

Research, or "auto-archeology," as I like to call it, is the key. Many museums, private collections, books, sales brochures, and photo histories are available. But I've found the best, not to mention, most rewarding way to research these delightful, historic machines is to go to an Antique Automobile Club of America (AACA) show. Every autumn in Hershey, Pennsylvania, at the Eastern Division AACA National Fall Meet, you can find acres and acres of antique and classic cars displayed in chronological order. These

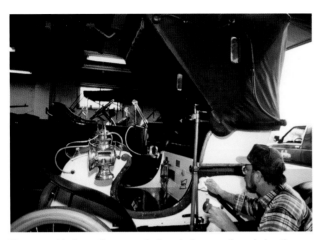

You can get to know the car and where to lay your lines during the preparation process as you eliminate any surface contaminates that would interfere with the striping.

This 1902 Rambler was an interesting combination of raised surfaces and belt moldings that needed to be studied to determine where to—and where *not* to—place the pinstriping.

beautiful restorations are juried and held to the most stringent of guidelines for authenticity and originality, down to the smallest details. Here, you can photograph and research first-hand rare cars that you may never see anywhere else in the world. I enjoy sitting on the curb with a cup of coffee in the early morning light as the cars drive in to park.

OWNER INFORMATION

Most owners of restored vehicles can provide useful information on the striping colors and placement details. After all, they have usually spent numerous hours researching their restoration projects. Working closely with a knowledgeable owner and restorer helps the pinstriper determine which

This one-of-a-kind 1929 Hebert-Darrin Custom Stutz has some great opportunities to get creative by carrying the interior motif onto the striping on the belt molding.

Striping next to the belt line was the method chosen to bring out the beauty of this 1903 Cadillac.

factor in a car's first impression. Heavy or thick pinstriping is typically incorrect and too massive for an antique car. Poor color choices or misplaced striping can ruin a beautiful restoration job. I have noticed that even museums, unfortunately, display poor examples of "era-correct" pinstriping in their collections. In my opinion, these examples exist due only to laziness or lack of knowledge. Antique and classic car pinstriping is nothing like contemporary "dealer striping," where you run down the side of a car, following a tape guide with your brush. Experience and lots of research are the best teachers in the quest of authentic auto-archeology.

John Walters' 1910 Packard Model 30, known as the "gentleman's run-a-bout," is a good example of how working closely with the owner in making decisions on striping details makes for a successful job. We pored over the only photos known to exist of two different 1910 Packard Model 30s. One car had details that were fairly accurate; the other was poorly striped with thick and thin gold tape. We had to make judgment calls on all the areas that we could not see in the photos. We agreed on the basic details, then we used a bit of artistic license for the missing sections. The result was continuity throughout the car. This elaborate job took several

information is correct and how to proceed with confidence. I've seen some horrible examples of incorrect striping that was either an afterthought or just a result of poor execution. Pinstriping is one of the first things you notice from afar. It is also the finishing touch that can end up being the major

Using the striping-hand ring finger on the bottom of the belt as a guide helps to keep a uniform distance from the edge of the belt molding.

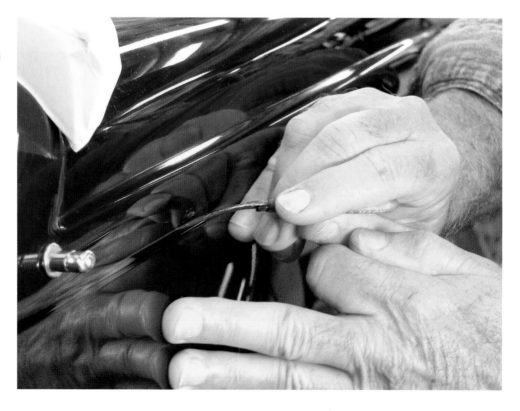

A finger is used as distance guide for a mock stripe laid on with Stabilo pencil.

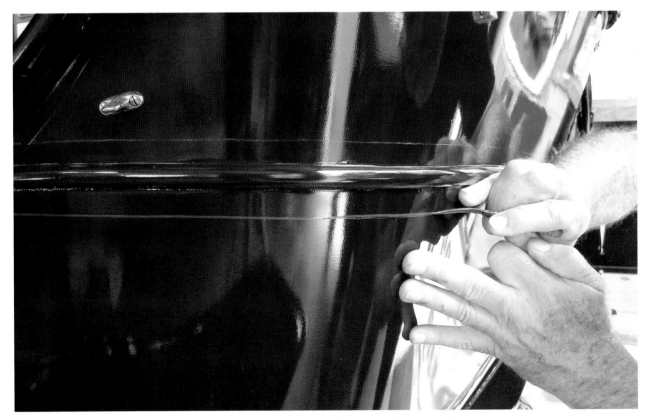

Striping follows the pencil line as a finger is used to maintain a consistent distance from the belt molding.

Before the development of improved pigments, metallic-bronze powders in a varnish base were used for brilliant gold effects. Later, more silver tones could be incorporated into the ornaments and pinstriping.

Light brings out the brilliance of the gold in the pinstripe. This sparkle is most evident as the car moves from shadows to full sunlight.

days to complete; there was pinstriping on almost every part of the running gear, frame, and body. I think the longest stripe I pulled was only 3 foot long. It was crucial that all of these short lines were consistent in width and that the numerous corners were crisp and sharp.

Color, as a rule, changes the mood and character of a car. Current styles and trends all play a roll in the final decision when choosing colors. This is another area where working with the owner is important. I have found that striping a variety of colors on a test panel is a good way for the owner to see what the stripe will look like on the car. Most people

This 1932 Auburn 12 boat-tail speedster is painted in a bold contrast of black and bright yellow. Special care is needed in mixing the color for the stripe so it is not overpowering.

have a hard time visualizing what the final results will look like. I like to get this out of the way prior to committing to fastidious jobs.

In situations where a collector might employ their spouse or young child when choosing paint options for their antique cars, I try to remain reasonably "open," keeping in mind that collectors go through color phases just like anyone else. I recall a job where the owner of a custom Packard painted a not-so-traditional mauve color handed me a swatch of dress material that his wife picked out for the pinstriping details. This delicate situation called for a fair amount of decorum, sprinkled with grace. In such cases I will often try to suggest a direction that accommodates the owner's personal tastes in addition to doing what is best for that particular car.

WHERE TO DRAW THE LINE

Start thinking about where you will place the stripe as you begin cleaning the car. Become familiar with all the details of the body construction as you wipe down the entire body (see Chapter 4). A good question to ask yourself during this process is: "Are the belt moldings lined up and consistent throughout the body?" Some early car bodies look like they have two different bodies combined together to make one. Becoming aware of all the car's unique body details during the preparation process can help you understand how the original striper may have reached the conclusion as to where to "draw the line." Typically the pinstripe is on the belt moldings if there are not too many

A thin pinstripe is imperative with this high-contrast color combination. A thicker stripe would have pushed the bold contrast too far.

Louvers can offer good guides for your fingers. I stripe from right to left to avoid contact with the previously painted stripes.

interruptions. Another option is to stripe next to the belt moldings. Overall consistency of the striping is the desired goal.

Wherever the stripe is to be painted, the method used in holding your brush is about the same. Your fingers will now become guides, measuring distances between the edges of the belt moldings and where you pull the stripe. It will take practice to train your hand to accommodate all circumstances, such as working around nonremovable accessories and transferring pressure to span door, hood, and panel gaps.

I use the two-handed or *over-handed* method, because no matter what direction I am striping—left, right, horizontal, or vertical—there is always a finger to guide the brush along the belt. When striping on the belt, I run my finger along the outer edge of the belt. When striping next to the belt, I like to make a mock stripe with a Stabilo first to be sure I like the placement. Then I choose a finger to become a guide, always measuring the stripe's distance from the belt. The space between the stripe and belt must remain consistent.

The pinstripe on the louver edge accents and highlights an otherwise flat area of this beautifully curved vehicle.

The finished hood sides can be carefully installed after the stripes are dry. Striping the hood sides before they are installed is a luxury I have with Stone Barn Automobile Restoration, as they are located close to my studio.

Some of the most interesting obstacles and challenges you will ever encounter are on Brass Era cars.

OBSTACLES

Obstacles such as carriage bolts, door handles, and latches need to be avoided if possible. Remove the items that you can as you encounter them when preparing the vehicle for striping. Some obstacles cannot be removed, which means you may have to paint with your "wrong" hand or in a direction that you are not accustomed to. Using taped guides and working in small sections can also be a solution in tight spots. Brass Era cars have some of the most unique obstacles you'll ever encounter. One of the most memorable that I've encountered was an ornate horn that resembled a snake.

Take extra time and patience to work around obstacles that cannot be removed. If you are in good communication with the restorer of the car, they will sometimes have you paint the tough spots as they assemble the vehicle. This is an optimum situation for painting difficult places. It is always best to relax, slow down, and learn about the unique hand-made characteristics of each vehicle as you go along. I have learned so much from this process and find that I enjoy imagining that I might be in the same frame of mind as the person who originally striped the car.

Patience is required to remove obstacles safely. You can learn how beauty followed function on these rolling works of art. Leather fenders are easily removed to access the body for striping this 1901 Knox. It is always interesting to discover the unusual construction of an antique automobile.

In some striping situations, using tape in tight spots may be the only way to solve hard-to-reach areas.

This 1903 Cadillac had to be striped after it was built, which opened up a world of challenges to be overcome creatively.

Here's a classic example of single-striping using white alongside black. Like a tuxedo, it is always in style.

You can achieve different star patterns on wooden spokes by varying the color, thickness, and closeness of each stripe.

WHEELS

Antique-wheel striping details vary from a simple single stripe to gold leaf with multiple color outlines. The early spoke wheels had several variations of a pointed arrow shape on each spoke. Arrows were thick at the hub and tapered to a point toward the rim. Other wheels had solid, colored arrows with outline stripes in a color that matched the striping on the body. Auto-archeology is always necessary to determine the proper characteristics and will make the difference between winners and losers.

Some hubs on early vehicles had multiple stripes, colors, and ornamentation and are real works of art. As steel rims were introduced, the styles changed to simpler striping

continued on page 93

Striping and spinning the wheels is impossible if the brakes are not adjusted to turn freely. I find striping the wheels before they are installed is much more efficient and produces more favorable results.

An arrow motif is carried out in outline form into the center of each spoke with a simple, yet dramatic line. Note how the hub also is encircled with a thin white line.

A clean edge is created for the arrows by using 1/4-inch tape at the base of the hub. You should pre-mark the length of each arrow with a Stabilo pencil.

This is a most fanciful wheel. The star pattern is created by painting each individual arrow radiating out from the hub, and is enhanced by the black mounting bolts at the center of each spoke. Function and form working together.

Adding two thin lines and another bold red line emphasizes this classic triple-striped Chevrolet wheel.

This original wheel with original color and paint has been a useful reference for creating authentic striping details when restoring wheels.

A 1910 Model T spoked wheel receives a simple-yet-authentic arrow stripe. This stripe should be ended just about an inch past the midpoint on each spoke.

Finding an original steel rim with multiple stripes is an invaluable reference for striping thickness and for spacing from the hub. Note how the stripe is perfectly interrupted by the air valve stem.

With photo information at hand, the outer stripe is lightly drawn on with a Stabilo pencil. I found a rubber washer that serves as a good guide.

Starting with the stripes on the hub and working out to the rim eliminates the chance of damaging the wet stripes. Tape is laid around the hub to give the arrows a clean edge.

The arrows are painted with the same striping brush. The left side of the arrow is outlined then the right. Next, the brush is reloaded and laid on its side to fill in the arrow.

continued from page 88
designs; some still continued to use the arrow shapes in outline forms. Others had stripes of various thicknesses and color encircling the entire rim.

Striping wheels while they are mounted on any car is always a challenge. If this is the only option, the car must be lifted and adjusted so the wheels turn freely. Early chain driven models make turning the wheels a struggle due to the excessive amount of moving parts that need to move to make the wheel spin. For the best results with these types of cars, remove the wheels or stripe them before the tires are mounted

My current method for striping wheels utilizes an old salvaged front wheel and axle from a mini-bike that I found in the barn. I mount the axle vertically in a vise, then I place the wheel to be striped on top of this state-of-the-art, homemade thing-a-ma-jig. Next, I spin the entire wheel slowly and lower the striping brush to the rim. For the best results and efficiency, I turn the wheel with my free hand while painting with the other.

Striping wheels and achieving good results is a challenge. In the past I have used everything from a phonograph turntable with adjustable speed control to a barstool. Whatever gives you the best result is the way to go.

continued on page 97

Finally the outer stripe is painted. As the wheel is spun, the brush is slowly dropped into position.

Above and below: The 1903 Packard here is one of only three known to exist and was the first Packard to make a coast-to-coast trip across the United States. The restoration shop supplied me with plenty of photo references and had the foresight to strip the running gear before assembly. You can imagine how difficult it would have been to stripe those parts afterward.

Both of the axles have a double stripe that wraps around from front to back. I use 1/8-inch fine-line tape as a layout guide to keep the space between the lines uniform and to give all the turns sharp, crisp corners. The stripe is run over the taped corners. When the tape is removed, the excess paint is removed along with it.

Above and left: Careful study of the 1903 Packard photos revealed many inaccuracies, but one commonality was the fine double stripes on all the running gear similar to those on horse-drawn carriages I have seen in several museums.

Left and below: After all the running gear and frame had been assembled, an appointment was made to finish all the rest of the body and fenders. The fenders were striped on a stand and assembled after the body was striped. Striping in stages means you need to mix the color each time you stripe or store enough premixed color in an airtight container.

The size 00 Mack Fast-Lite brush is designed to replace the Grumbacher 000, which is no longer available.

continued from page 93
BRUSH SELECTION
The right brush to use is determined by the length of the lines, the sharpness of the turns, and the curves and shape of the car. For long thin lines I choose a size 1, 2, or 3 Fast-Lite by the Mack Brush Company. For shorter lines or tight turns, a shorter, more flexible brush is in order, like the size 000 Mack Series 10, or the Xcaliber size 0000 These brushes work great tight turns, and their bellies don't kick out as you turn corners. But as I've said before, the brush that works best for the job is the one you feel most comfortable using.

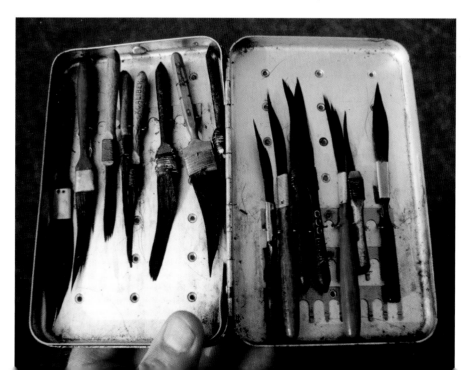

This modified aluminum fly tackle box in which I store assorted brushes was a gift from a friend.

A paint swatch guide placed over a fender makes choosing a color easier for you and the customer.

COLOR CHOICE

Robert Turnquist, the founder and owner of Hibernia Auto Restorations in New Jersey, states in his comprehensive book *The Packard Story* that "Color is a wonderful tool and, used carefully, will make a beautiful classic even more beautiful." A careful study in color theory is essential to successfully harmonize striping to reflect the character of a classic car. Custom-built cars could be painted any color combination from the 1,305 colors that were available in 1932. This color palette gave customers great latitude when it came to choosing a color to suit a particular taste. The pinstriping color can detract or complement the desired mood of the car.

First and most difficult is the starting point. This area cannot be done later without touching wet paint. Reaching as far as you can enables you to start the line at a point you can reach easily from the opposite side of the car.

Front and rear cowls are striped to break points at the hood and doors. Never leave a stripe dry in the middle of a panel, as it will be more difficult to blend the stripes together.

The bottom stripe of the top belt molding is tackled after the top stripe has been completed. Working top to bottom helps ensure you do not get into the wet stripes.

I've found that a winning combination includes a finely striped line and a subtle complementary color that reflects a sense of calm and richness. This sometimes translates into a subtle tone-on-tone or monotone body-and-stripe combination.

I recall that the owner of the 1934 Custom Packard Dietrich Model 1108 convertible sedan shown here wanted a slightly brighter tone of the body color that was barely visible indoors, but which appeared as a highlight when it was out in the sunlight, which is the way it is supposed to look. To find a suitable color solution I used a color sample book from an automotive paint supplier; these samples have a hole cut in each color chip that allows you to see through to the paint of the car when the chart is placed on the surface.

After careful preparation to remove any contaminants, I start from the top and work my way down to avoid running into any wet paint. Beginning with the front cowl I stripe both lines, reaching over as far as possible and connecting

For crisp points and corners, overlap ends and carefully wipe off the excess. Use this technique on all sharp corners for a clean finished look. But remember: this can only be done easily if the first stripe has dried sufficiently.

Lower belt moldings are the biggest challenge because they are tough to reach and it can be difficult to see. Simply run a length of tape and follow it through.

A masking tape guide can control uneven edges, such as convertible tops. This is a good example of an uneven section that can be smoothed out by following a guide.

Striping the "other way" is necessary when confronted with obstacles and tight spots. You should try striping with either hand so you are ready for this kind of situation.

each side ending at a break point, in this case the hood and door. Next, paint the top stripe around the upper belt molding and hood, followed by the bottom stripe of the upper belt molding to completion.

If you encounter hard-to-get-at places such as the rear or an uneven convertible top, use tape as a guide and run the stripe as close as possible to the tape. In some cases you'll find it easier to stripe in the opposite direction at these points. Clean off any mistakes with your rag and surface cleaner as you go, and create crisp overlaps such as points on the hood.

Now we move down to the bottom belt molding, which starts and ends at the hood bottom. The hood sides can be tough to stripe. After you mark where the stripe crosses the hood, unlatch the hood sides and carefully lift the sides out and up to a comfortable height. Have someone from the shop do this or help you rest the bottom edge on a soft but rigid block of foam rubber that doesn't get in the way of the stripes.

For the fenders you need something comfortable to crawl around on, like a piece of foam rubber or a moving

Run the stripe past break points, wiping off the excess as you go. For quick cleanups, always have a rag and a squirt bottle of reducer ready.

The finished front fender points. Let everything dry as you move to the lower section of the car.

A comfortable pad is necessary when lying down to stripe lower regions; in this case the bottom of the front fender.

blanket. You can't do good work in bad conditions. On that note, with a color this subtle, you need as much light as you can get, which is why I moved this job out in the natural light, but not in the direct sun.

This is a real sit-down job. The best part—the rear fenders—are a nice break from the "straight and narrow."

Get yourself seated comfortably and at the right height to be able to reach both the starting and the ending points. Next, palette the paint to the proper consistency. Reach over, touching just the tip of the brush to the bottom edge, and go all the way over to the bottom of the other side in one shot,

continued on page 105

Find the center point of the rear fender by sitting at a comfortable level and centering yourself so you easily can reach both ends of the fender and the top. Your body is like the center of a compass.

Hood sides must be lifted so that you can stripe their bottoms. They are also tricky without the proper support. The hood will shake and it will be impossible to do any decent striping. Special care must be taken to prevent damaging bodywork. Do not try moving parts without help from the shop crew.

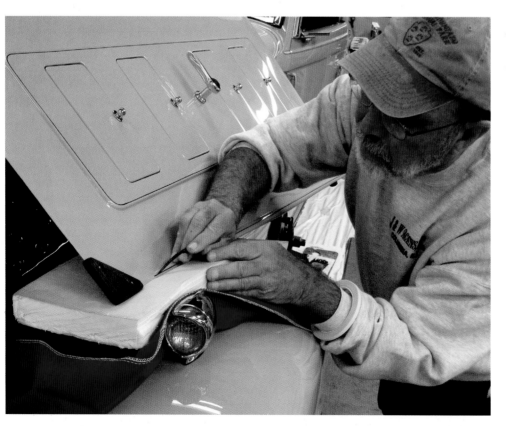

A foam support for a hood side has to be rigid enough so you can stripe without hitting it.

This is how these double stripes are finished off at this particular front fender ending point. Special attention must be used to ensure both fenders end at exactly the same point.

There is no room for errors when working white on black. This is the best hand position I have found to work the round rear fenders. As I run around the fender I change which finger I use to steady my hand.

A finished double striped rear section with all the sharp turns negotiated.

Some customers prefer their initials or coat of arms painted on each side of the vehicle. Keep these small and refined.

The natural wood belt moldings on this 1901 Knox led me to locate the stripes off the belt molding and to use some unusual brush-handling methods.

Corners have to be squared off nicely for a sharp appearance. Paint the stripe past the corners, then wipe off the excess toward the corners.

continued from page 101

using your finger as a guide on the edge of the fender. After you have both stripes, finish them off to the running boards. Use the same technique on the front fenders to a point, making sure both front fenders are exactly the same.

Now that wasn't so bad, was it? But this is a 1934 12-cylinder Dietrich model that was given the double-stripe treatment; that means you're going around again right next to the stripes you just finished.

Now you have two choices, depending on how you feel or how rushed the job is. And believe me, you don't want to rush, so: 1) You can go to lunch and then come back and finish it very carefully because you can't wipe off any new mistakes very easily if the first stripe is still soft, or, 2) You can come back tomorrow and finish after you've caught a few trout on the way home and let the first set of stripes get good and dry.

CHAPTER 9
HOT RODS AND CUSTOMS

Earlier this year, while I was waiting for paint to dry at Dave Crouse's garage in Loveland, Colorado, I had the opportunity to pick his brain a little about hot rod history as he finished hooking up a 427 engine in a beautiful '32 Ford, three-window coupe. I don't know anyone who knows more than Dave regarding who built what car and where it is today. He is a first-rate auto-archeologist. As always, I found myself enjoying a trip down memory lane with Dave as I had the opportunity to stripe another great roadster that he and the guys at Custom Auto built. This is some of what we talked about between pinstripes and big blocks.

Prior to World War II, souped-up Model Ts with overhead-valve conversions and four-cylinder Chevys with Olds heads, were among the first "gow jobs" to run flat-out on the dry lakes of California. Postwar production cars were being modified for speed in numbers like never before.

During the early 1950s, these hot rods, as they were nicknamed, took to the streets, unfortunately gaining a negative reputation in the press and in movies. Organized drag racing, with an emphasis on safety, gradually helped these vehicles and their owners gain acceptance.

I met Dave Crouse when he worked at Stone Barn Automobile Restoration in Great Meadows, New Jersey, where I striped. One day he asked me, "Do you know how to do striping like Ed Roth?" I guess he thought I only did the "straight stuff." I striped his '32 Ford coupe in exchange for a set of fenders for the 1946 Chevy pickup I was building. More than 15 years later, he called to tell me he was in Colorado and wished I was around to stripe for him. It turns out his shop is in the same town where my sons and grandkids are! We had a lot of catching up to do.

The *Highland Plating Special* roadster has been photographed in many configurations. Here I lettered it as it appeared in its drag-racing days. There are not many vintage photos of it in this mode.

In the 1960s, these glorious machines—newly named "street rods"—represented a newfound symbol of freedom and mobility. The street rod was more refined to fit each driver's personality, style and means. In the late 1960s, performance ruled, and muscle cars became the new showroom, turnkey hot rods. You just dropped into a dealership, signed your name on the dotted line, and drove away in a brand-new tire-smoker. However, these stylish pavement pounders still needed to be customized to suit the individual owners' taste.

By the late 1970s, street rods were being built with all the latest technology in suspension, performance, and comfort. Each custom-built vehicle was a symbol of the owner's style and personality. Doctors and lawyers were now able to drive a custom-built, reliable, new/old cool car. Predictably, the prices went through the roof.

Custom painters of that era, who had always been involved with car culture, found a new boom in business: painting individual paint schemes to capture the customer's one-of-a-kind self-expression. Today, the street rod business is bigger than ever, with no sign of slowing anytime soon. Retiring baby-boomers are buying the cars they were not able to afford when they were teenagers. Newfound mobile nostalgia and the means to cruise the country fuel this phenomenon. Investing in these cars, rather than putting money in the stock market, is proving not just a good investment, but also an investment you can enjoy driving. The low-brow social outcast vehicle of the past is now a collectable and valued investment.

Hot rods with documented histories have become valued additions to serious automotive collections. This documentation is as important as matching numbers are to a muscle car. Restoration of these historic vehicles began during the 1960s, with cars like the *Highland Plating Special* 1925 *continued on page 111*

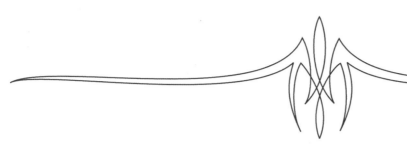

I like to stripe the most difficult parts of a car first. In the case of the Berardini Bros. "404 Jr." roadster, which was being restored at Dave Crouse's Custom Auto, I began the majority of the pinstriping on the sides of the hood and the top.

While I was still in the louver mood, I finished the rear deck. After pinstriping all these louvers, everything else was an adventure into the head of Von Dutch, who laid the car's original stripes in 1953.

When the lettering was completed, the hood was reassembled. The white pinstriping had some unusual starting and ending points that really puzzled me. Although photo history is crucial to any type of restoration job, I was allowed some artistic license, but not much. I had to force myself to add the random pinstriping inlines halfway down the numbers, to comply with the integrity of the restoration.

Further research into the only photo evidence available for us to work from revealed some clues. The front fenders were similar to those of any BMW motorcycle. Knowing Dutch's familiarity with motorcycles, the reasons for why he did what he did on the "404 Jr." began to make sense.

The rear-fender pinstriping just ended for no particular reason, but using the photo evidence, I had to conform exactly to what Von Dutch did on the original paint job.

There were no photos of the dash, so as scary as it may seem, I jumped in, thought "Dutch," and forgot about everything (except the extra-large beer I was going to have in his honor if I made it through the job unscathed).

My head is spinning, trying to figure out why Dutch painted some of these things the way he did. It really was a challenge and at times it didn't make sense to me. So I stopped thinking so much and decided to outline another letter to forget. When I thought I was finished, I noticed an "inline" that appeared inside the lettering. This line seemed random because it just stopped halfway down the number. I thought of four or five possibilities for the apparent disconnect, none of them comforting. All those reference photos that showed these details now haunted me.

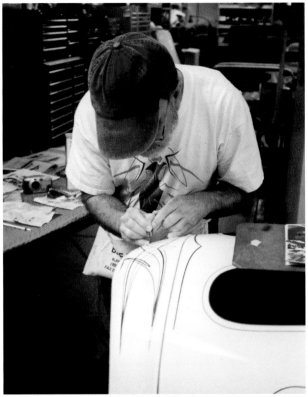

The striping on the hood and grille shell was a real challenge, mainly because there was only one 3/4 photo for reference, and it was blurry. I sketched out what was visible and straightened it out. After striping the crowning touches on the hood and grille shell, we all went out for that beer. It's not easy getting back *out* of Dutch's head. I gained a new respect for his work.

continued from page 107
roadster and others. Some of these cars have vast archives of photo reference to help with the restoration; others don't.

Recently, I had the pleasure of researching, pinstriping, and lettering the Berardini Bros. "404 Jr." 1932 roadster, is one of the most famous continually raced cars in the history of drag racing. Von Dutch did the original pinstriping in the early 1950s. It was a complete restoration job—also in Dave Crouse's shop—of a one-of-a-kind race car.

The photos of the original "404 Jr." showed evidence of some details that were fairly crude by today's standards. Some latitude was given to me and I employed a bit of artistic license for improvements. The car currently resides in one of two locations: the NHRA Wally Parks Motorsport Museum in Pomona, California, or in Roger Morrison's private collection.

INTERNATIONAL KUSTOM CAR CULTURE

Recently, while I was over in Finland attending a pinhead/American car show, I couldn't help noticing how much our kustom culture has influenced the enthusiastic car builders there. On a garage tour, we saw mostly "low-buck" cars that are built to reliable, safe standards. Of course, there is nothing inexpensive about building an American car overseas. Imagine how hard it must be to find vintage American parts in Finland.

The get-in-and-drive mentality is alive and well overseas. I believe there are more hot rods in Sweden than in all of Europe. These Nordic hot rodders are among the boldest I

I was glad I did those inline stripes too, because Pat Berardini (right) told me how and why they were originally painted—it's a story that will remain safe with me.

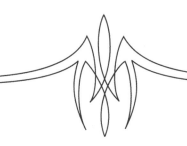

In Finland, builders take their work seriously. Here at the Road Pilots car club garage, you would think you were back in the States. The shop is located under an apartment building.

ever encountered. They drive in all kinds of weather, in spite of strict government restrictions (sound familiar?).

This attitude is shining bright back here in the States as well. The resurgence can be witnessed, coast-to-coast, in a whole new generation of so-called "rat rodders" building cars. The negative connotation is reminiscent of the early 1950s, as hot rod history repeats itself. The fact that "rat rods" are built with *real* scrounged parts and not with 1-800-PARTs means that the owners mostly home-build them, typically with a little help from their friends. Money can't buy everything—especially when it comes to a hand-built hot rod.

I recall a rainy day at the National Street Rod Association Street Rod Nationals in York, Pennsylvania, where the drivers with their "rat rods" were cruisin' in the mud and rain, loving every minute of it, while the owners of show cars hid their vehicles in trailers.

Pinstriping seems to be the vehicle art of choice with many rat rodders. I have noticed that many try their own hand at pinstriping their cars. It's great to see this art created by someone who just picks up a brush and has at it.

HOW TO WORK A CAR SHOW

If all your friends think you have what it takes and you have a good body of work to prove it, here are some things you should know.

Before you go out in public to pinstripe at a car or bike show, you should have been striping for a fair amount of time. You should have mastered the brush and paint, and you should be equipped for the variety of tasks that you will be asked to perform. Be sure of your capabilities as a pinstriper so you are not embarrassed and become discouraged.

Start out slow, perhaps with a local cruise night. Then try a small local show where you can surround yourself with some of your customers and their cars for support and to show examples of your real work. You must learn to be comfortable working in front of crowds in conditions that are less than

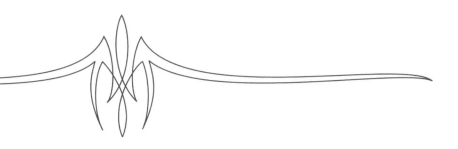

In spring 2006 we stopped by the Pistons car club on our Finland garage tour to see some cool cars. Check out the Edsel grille on that coupe. Jonna Leskinen is a new pinstriper who is doing some great work.

ideal, juggling questions about pricing and handling money, while you work. You should be able to maintain a good attitude and roll with anything that comes your way.

In my high school days I striped all of my friends' cars in the neighborhood, and then I striped cars in the high school parking lot at lunch. In theory, I graduated from the Ronald McDonald School of Nighttime Pinstriping; I received a major in cheeseburgers and chocolate shakes, and a minor in parking-lot striping and street racing. I received my masters from the Circus Cruise-Thru Institute of Asbury Park.

I eventually felt confident enough to start painting at the Raceway Park drag strip at Englishtown, New Jersey, on opening day. I learned quickly how to work fast on cars in the staging lanes. I lettered up my '57 Chevy with shoe polish for advertising, then I raced down the quarter-mile. On the return road I would stop at the timing tower and ask

The only cars driving around in the rain at this NSRA event in York, Pennsylvania, were "rat rodders." Their spirits were not dampened by a little wetness, but we had a hard time keeping cars dry enough to work on them.

With its black primer, striped grille insert and air cleaner, Von Dutch flying eyeball on the cowl, and adequate coating of road dust, this roadster is a prime example of the "rat rod" aesthetic.

Vinnie Napp if he would announce that I was working in the pits. He always was happy to do it. What a cool guy he was.

VENDOR APPLICATIONS AND FEES

These fees are usually paid up front, ahead of the show. Fees can range from zero to well over $1,000, depending on the size and scale of the event. The larger shows require a state tax ID number that you must apply for way ahead if you are an out-of-state-resident. At any time you can get an unannounced visit from "The Friendly Show Taxman," which can be a

hassle, so keep it legal. Some cities have other licenses and fees to deal with, too. Welcome to the show game.

INSURANCE

Having insurance is required at larger shows and it is always a good thing to have, especially when the wind lifts the tent off the ground in an otherwise peaceful day, over a priceless car. Our shop insurance covers us for all such problems at shows away from home. Check with your insurance agent and gain peace of mind, so you can just paint.

After honing my skills in the school parking lot, I felt confident enough to start painting at the Raceway Park drag strip at Englishtown, New Jersey. The night before the drags, I would sneak a couple of Mom's oil-painting brushes and some white shoe polish to letter up my '57 Chevy as advertising. Old English–style letters were the easiest.

The quarter-mile drags were great for shaking up the paint just right for a day of striping and lettering. But then the linkage fork ring would blow off the transmission synchronizer barrel, usually caused by a high-revving 283 followed by a flawless power shift. This would leave me with only first or third gear to limp back home to a late night of transmission repair to get to work in the morning.

A 20x20-foot tent is just the ticket to work on two cars at one time. You can mentally design a paint scheme on one car while you finish the other. Even at a small show you should bring enough signage so people can find you. You never know where you will be setting up.

SETUP AND DISPLAY

Most shows allow vendors to set up a day or so before the public is allowed in. Vendor spaces are typically marked off in 10-foot sections. I rent a 20x20-foot space. This allows me room to set up my large show tent and work on two cars at the same time. One car can be prepped or cooling off while I finish up another. You can invest in your own tent or, if available, rent one and have it set up for you at the show.

continued on page 119

We arrive at shows loaded down with everything and then some. You can hear the circus music in your head as you start setting up the "big top."

If you have ever had a pair of shoes that were just perfect, you know how you can get used to something that just fits you perfectly. I don't have to think about where something is with this faithful setup. Ron, a woodworker at a local marina, did a splendid job on the truck's mahogany and oak woodwork. He designed it to fit together as if it was a Chris-Craft. The truck blends into the marina while I am gold-leafing boats there.

I have fond memories of working with my sons as we built this truck together from the frame up.

The wood-graining carries the mahogany color and grain pattern inside. This technique is not very difficult to learn—my sons did most of it with a piece of a rag.

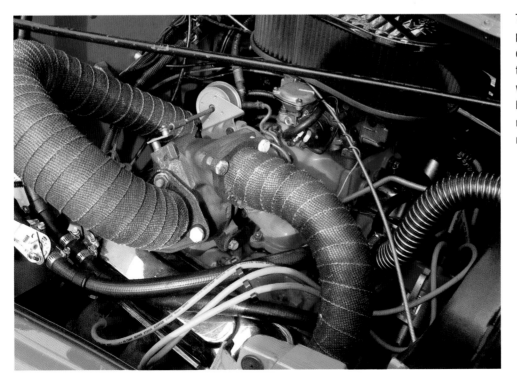

The V-6 Buick turbo provides motivation with exhilaration no matter what the load. And with four-wheel drive and air shocks, hauling a full load of hay is no problem with this multifunctional truck.

Gold leaf and my logo design communicate the nature of my work simply and to the point.

The faux-wood belt molding fools a lot of people at the shows. They slowly move closer to see if those screws are real. I have to paint an old rusty, bent nail on the molding somewhere just for fun

This color selection method is the best thing I have found to help the customer decide on colors. The colors on the chart can be mixed to suit even the most particular spouse. Before I found this method I had to post a sign that read, "Husbands are required to have a note from their spouse to choose colors."

When used to describe pinstriping, "Von Dutch" or "old-school" refers to loose, free-form, and heavy striping that is not subtle in color or design. On a flat-black vehicle, a design of this style is typically done in red and white. Modern colors, like magenta, teal, or pastels are rarely, if ever used. Old-school jobs are great because you don't have to get your work so tight—you can just let go and have fun without a safety net. I tend to add a little purple to my red to mellow it a bit. I also throw some brown into my ivory to keep the two color values in harmony.

continued from page 115

SIGNAGE

Visually, your signage should reflect the kind of work you do. It should be clear and legible from a long distance. I have three banners that I affix to my tent and which display in all directions the words "PINSTRIPING & GRAFIX" in bold and large letters. Don't get too fancy with your signs. Remember, when it comes to readability, contrast is king! You can dazzle them with all your goodies once they find you in the crowd.

PHOTO ALBUMS

In front of your tent or space, set up a portable table with photo albums containing quality photos of your work laid on it. It is good to have another sign on this table, visually reinforcing your skills. Customers will look through your work and hopefully find something they like. Some stripers have elaborate samples of graphics and styles displayed. I prefer not to give people too much to choose from. I believe it slows the decision-making process when there is too much information to sort out.

Now the pricing game will begin, as showgoers point to a photo and ask, "How much does that cost?" We have a $50 minimum charge for anything we paint no matter how small. This eliminates little jobs that could pile up when the cars are lined up waiting for you get to them (but more on pricing later in this chapter).

Tribal pinstriping has sharp, pointed, abrupt right-angle turns and is typically painted using vivid colors that tend to be on the dark side. No happy, smiley colors will do. This is tribal striping with a bit of Southwestern flare added in.

Mild or subtle pinstriping is done with monotone or low-contrast, complementary colors. This '32 grille shell is a simple combination of gray and a lighter tone of blue. You have to know when to stop—more is not always better.

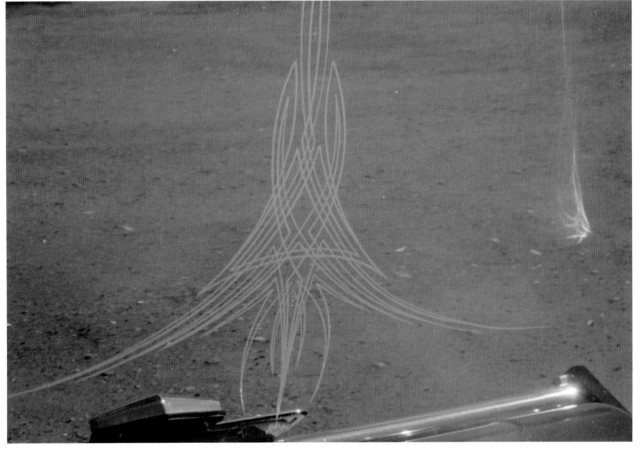

Subtle can be achieved in a number of ways. A very dark maroon creates a very low contrast that is barely visible in shade, but striking in full sun.

PAINTS, BRUSHES, AND SUPPLIES

I have a show checklist of what has to be packed that I use over and over again. This list is always being updated, but it serves as a flawless tool when you have preshow jitters. Just as a chef in a busy kitchen needs everything close at hand, it is important not to waste time looking for what might have gotten left behind in the 5 a.m. mad dash to get on the road.

Speed, preparation, and organization are the keys to having a successful show. I have 40 years' experience working shows on the road, and I still love to work out of my custom-built 1946 Chevy pickup truck, using the same paint box that I work out of in my studio. I know where everything is and that doesn't change.

I traded a full-tilt lettering and graphics job on a race car for the truck, which had been beat up pretty badly by more then one owner with big ideas. Actually, come to think of it, almost everything on or in that truck was traded for. I needed to find a better frame and running gear. I stumbled upon a rolled-over 1979 Toyota 4x4 at a junkyard. It looked like it was about the right size, so I traded sign-lettering services for the Toyota.

Finding parts was a memorable adventure with my sons, Eric and Chris. They learned a lot about cars through that experience. They even wood-grained the dash with me.

The two-tone colors I chose closely resemble orange and brown M&Ms. It must be because my old studio was in Hackettstown, New Jersey, home of Mars, Incorporated, the makers of M&Ms. Everyone that came to my studio during the painting process asked, "Is that the color it's going to be?" Or, "Are you going to leave it that color?" I have found that you are much better off *not* listening to many opinions when it comes to the beginning stages of a paint project, unless you spell out for them everything that you are planning. Trends

Wild striping designs are generally painted with multiple, high-contrast colors. This style can be as large or as busy as the customer desires. Nothing exceeds like excess, I always say.

come and go but class is timeless. I know several painters who have redone their shop trucks many times to keep up with the current trends. My old lacquer paint is still shiny enough for me.

I traded services for the design and building of the truck's wood bed with a woodworker at a marina that specializes in wooden-boat restorations. Now, I do all their gold-leaf work.

Air shocks for the extra weight carried to the shows and an air tank and compressor from a Cadillac for the airbrush work fine. Cranking out the front windshield provides factory air-conditioning. My original purposes for building the truck were to advertise the type of work I specialize in and to use it daily for work. (Although the four-wheel-drive and Buick V-6 Turbo

power come in handy for hauling hay for the animals.) My truck is a customer conversation piece that serves as additional advertising of my work. My logo is gold-leafed on both doors, with additional, subtle trick-paint techniques, such as faux wood grain painted on the belt moldings.

PEOPLE BARRIERS

Flags or caution tape can be strung around the tent to keep overcurious visitors out of your work area when it gets very busy. The last thing you need is someone running his or her fingers through a freshly striped car, saying "Golly, that *is* wet paint!" Believe it or not, it has happened. I only use this territorial barrier when it is absolutely necessary. I like to remain approachable for questions and conversation.

WIND BARRIERS AND OTHER COMFORTS

Screened tent sidewalls are available that can quickly be put up on windy days. Wind can blow the brush around and these sidewalls can cut the wind down substantially. You will discover that you may want to bring other comforts with you when working outdoors, such as foam rubber knee mats to use on those low jobs. You can sometimes find these mats and other cool stuff from fellow vendors at the show.

THE WAITING GAME

After your tent and displays are set up, you are ready to paint. Just like fishing, sometimes they're biting, sometime they're not. Waiting for things to happen can be nerve-wracking and full of insecurity and doubt. Instead of getting caught up in negativities, take this time to make friends with your neighbors, fellow vendors, and competitors. I've worked shows with three or four other stripers and we've had a blast joking and busting each other. Keep a good positive attitude; people don't want to have their car striped by a negative sourpuss. Having fun with people is the most important thing about working a show, making new friends and seeing faces you have not seen in a while.

By the way, I have never been stuck with a bad check from a customer at a hot rod show. Most car folks are the salt-of-the-earth and always ready to offer a helping hand. I'm proud to have had so many memorable years working with these first-class people.

LISTENING TO CUSTOMERS

No matter what verbal terms or visual reference the customer uses to describe what he or she wants painted, pay close

attention. Learn to read between the lines! Some people will use terms like *tribal*, *old-school*, *wild*, or *mild* to explain a direction for you to take in designing a look for their car. But first, you both need to agree on the definition of specific terms, to make sure you are on the same page.

Body language is another clue to what's inside the customer's head. I tend to watch carefully at the customer's hands and arm gestures, especially when it comes to the size of a design or graphic. If the customer suggests a small design on the deck lid and proceeds to stretch his hands from the top to bottom or from side-to-side, this situation calls for clarification on the size of the design to be painted.

I have a good friend and customer, Skipp Phelps, who is a mysterious collector of unique cars. We joke about customer psychology whenever he drops off a new car to be striped at my shop. He jokingly grimaces and says, "Fix-it. . . . I want something small," while stretching his arms as far as he can. He'll continue with, "You know, something smooth and flowing," as he makes jagged, sharp, erratic chopping motions with his hands. Skipp and I have always had a language all our own; he knows that no matter what he describes (in all seriousness), I will interpret it correctly and execute something that is exactly want he wanted, and more importantly, what the car needed.

Customer interpretation is an art form in and of itself. I have come to the conclusion that most customers think in a linear way and most artists think in a multidimensional way. Always be aware that you may need to make a responsible suggestion of what is best for the car. When a person says, "I want something subtle," immediately look at the car's colors, shape, and style while bearing in mind the customer's style of dress and possibly other personal traits. Reading between the lines can be very helpful in maintaining a good perspective of what the customer is really expressing to you, the artist.

Once you have gathered as much information as possible, you're on your way. Reaching a clear understanding at the beginning of any design project will make the painting part a joyful experience for both you and your customer.

COLOR AND STYLE SELECTION

NEVER use a color without showing a sample to the customer first. I sometimes go so far as putting a swatch of the paint color directly on the car. This can easily be removed and can play an invaluable part in the customer committing to a color choice. I have learned that people, in general, have a hard time envisioning the final product.

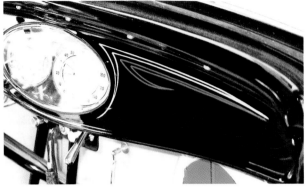

Simple old-school, clean and simple, not overdone. Dashboard striping has helped me cover expenses more than I can remember. This dash had an imperfection in the paint that could be hidden by some striping, which is how striping all began, you know.

Here is a simple method I've found that works well and which gives the customer a look at the colors before you start. I place color swatches from a vinyl color chart into a clear plastic 8 1/2x11-inch sleeve that neatly fits in my photo binder. I hold or tape the color chart onto the cars surface. This way the customer can see what colors actually look best on their cars. Once colors have been selected and clearly marked, we have eliminated the unknown and there should not be any misunderstandings.

CAR CHARACTER AND COLOR

The character of a hot rod is very different from that of a classic Brass Era vehicle or Packard, for example. All hot rods possess individual attitudes and personalities. For instance, a wild, radically chopped red coupe with a blown 1,000-horsepower mill sticking through the hood requires shocking, high-contrast colors. On a red car I would choose teal, blue, and/or slime green. This high contrast of color adds to and can bring out the beast in this vivid creation. A completely different color approach should be taken with a mild "resto rod" with nostalgic touches, even if it's painted in the same red. A more traditional color approach of ivory, gray, black, and/or white would be more suited to the car's character and bring out its old-school charm and style.

Choosing the correct color combinations for the car's and owner's characters creates a unique look that's harmonious with the owner and the car. Historically, hot rods have always been known to be custom-built to suit the individual owner's specifications and particular tastes.

I can remember this car when it was a basket case for sale in the car-parts area at a show.

Studying car and motorcycle history and learning how to recognize the subtleties of a particular vehicle will also help reveal the direction to go, which will in turn guide you down the correct path. More than anything else, the correct combination will result in a clean, classic, rich, mellow look. Pinstriping belt moldings and using a subtle, low-contrast or monotone color combination quietly brings out the beauty that is already present. There is an expertise in accenting a vehicle's true character. This can be done lightly or boldly, depending on the amount of contrast you choose.

RAIN AT A SHOW

Rain at a show can really put a damper on your day and a hole in your pocket. It is hard to make up the loss of business, not to mention your personal expenses, if you get rained out. We usually keep a sharp eye on the weather a week or so before a show, to be completely prepared for any conditions. If the weather does turn out to be bad, we book smaller jobs that can be done under the tent, where it is relatively dry. Some good projects for those rainy days are helmets, motorcycle fenders, and dashboards. We always assess jobs, taking weather conditions and drying time into consideration. If one day of a three-day show predicts rain, we try to book "tent jobs" for that day.

IMITATING OTHER STRIPERS ART

Copying designs of other stripers is a touchy subject and an ethical choice you have to make for yourself. On occasions a customer will bring a photo from a magazine or website of something they want reproduced on their car. Significantly modifying the art is the only way to handle this problem. Once, a guy showed me some art from a car magazine that he wanted me to reproduce precisely. I started to laugh as he showed it to me because it was a piece I originally painted on

Judy and I believe that whom God has blessed abundantly, much is expected. We try to work at various charity events throughout the year as a way of giving back in a small way. Judy also paces my day so I can still have fun. I don't know how you could work a show like this on your own without help and support.

that car for that magazine! If a customer becomes demanding, I ask them how they would feel if they saw someone else driving around with their custom design painted by someone else.

HOW MUCH DOES IT COST?

Another area where a complete understanding needs to be reached up front is regarding exactly what you will and will not do for the agreed-to price. Exact fees should always be agreed upon between the artist and the customer BEFORE you start the job. If the customer chooses to add additional pinstriping or painting once a job has started, you must clearly state that there will be additional charges. I usually stop and make sure I have the customer's full attention and explain that the request for additional work requires additional costs.

When a customer asks, "How much will it cost?" for a specific job, I use a ballpark figuring system that is based on a two-tier pricing method. This method is a good way to narrow down pricing with your customer.

After listening, and studying both the car and the customer, I initially come up with the first-tier price. This price is based on what I would do to accent and complement the car's beauty and character without financial limitations

placed on me by the customer. Generally this is the top end of the price structure. Next, I think of what would be the least amount of work I could do and still accent the car properly. This gives me the low price or second tier. It all boils down to the customer; he or she needs to decide which way to go to fit his or her budget. Of course the ideal customer is the one who brings in a vehicle and tells you to "Do what ever you think looks good," and doesn't blink an eye when you hand him the bill.

Finally, I never work busy car shows by myself. My amazing wife, Judy, handles all the details of pricing and customer appointments. Judy is also an artist who is experienced in color theory and design. She helps sort out the basic selections by conducting a quick interview regarding budget, design, and color choice. Judy and I met in art school. She majored in fashion illustration and is well-equipped to handle color and design questions. With Judy running interference and being efficient at weeding out tire-kickers, it leaves me worry-free to concentrate on designing and painting effectively. I can't imagine producing any kind of quality work at a major car show by myself. Her exhaustive eye for details and the big picture makes me actually look like I know what I'm doing.

CHAPTER 10
MOTORCYCLES

The major difference between pinstriping motorcycles and cars is the physical size of the area to be striped. For this reason, when working on a motorcycle, you need to stripe more delicately. Good motorcycle pinstriping is thinner than what you generally see on cars and trucks. These designs are also more complex, using tighter striping. After all, if it's a tank design, the customer is going to be looking down at the design for a long time. The symmetry must be dead-on, accurate, and crisp, and excellent line quality needs to be maintained throughout the design.

The type of motorcycle is another consideration that will determine the choice of design. The contrast in owner

With motorcycles tanks, you need to make your striping designs a little more intricate because the surface area is smaller and it will be right under the rider's nose for a long time to come. This tighter work is more time-consuming and should be reflected in the pricing.

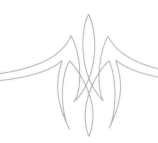

This is a typical Honda Gold Wing striping job. A rich maroon and a mid-tone gray is a safe way to make the conservative owner smile with satisfaction.

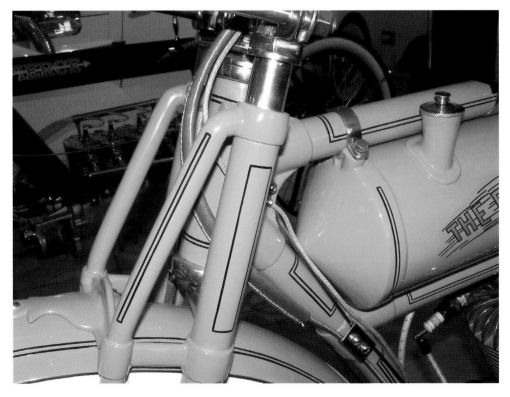

Notice the fine-line striping on this beautiful restored Merkel. If this striping, laid by a striper unknown to me, was heavier it would have ruined the entire look of this antique motorcycle.

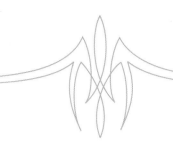

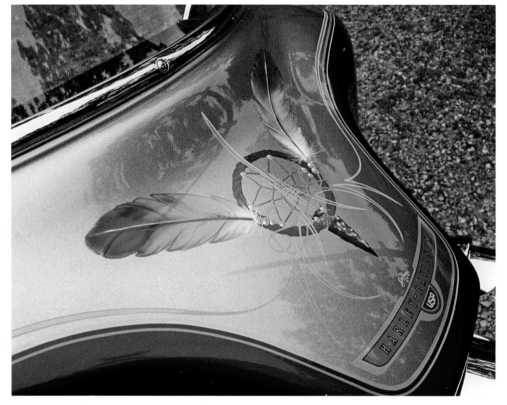

I was a bit surprised when a Harley owner wanted this dream-catcher design that, in my experience, a Gold Wing owner would be more inclined to choose. He explained he needed something a bit larger to hide a scratch on one side of the faring.

Keep the design simple and flowing with the shape of the bike. Figure out a price for each spot so the customer knows what they can afford. A design can be modified to fit their budget before you begin.

personality is more extreme between owners of different makes and styles of motorcycles than it is with car owners. The Harley-Davidson Fat Boy owner is usually quite different from the Honda Gold Wing owner. It's not like Ford versus Chevy here—it's an entirely different demographic. I do not recommend setting up at a Gold Wing rally with nothing but skulls and flames to offer. If you do, you will spend most of your time kicking rocks in the parking lot.

It is essential that as a pinstriper, you understand the differences among all of your customers. Whether they bring you an antique Indian, a custom-built Harley chopper, or a sportbike, countless problems can be averted by understanding the specific kind of motorcycle they own and carefully listening to their ideas about what they are interested in having you stripe. For the proper overall look to be achieved, this is critical in the selection of color and design.

The owner of this Kawasaki wanted a design that was not too wild. The job called for a color combination that included the existing factory accent colors used elsewhere on the bike and on the logo.

Kenny Duda's hardtail gets the old-school treatment. Kenny is the lead singer and guitar player in The Razorbacks rockabilly band.

You can't miss with a simple teardrop touch that says "old school."
Just a simple accent of color in the right spots makes a big impression.

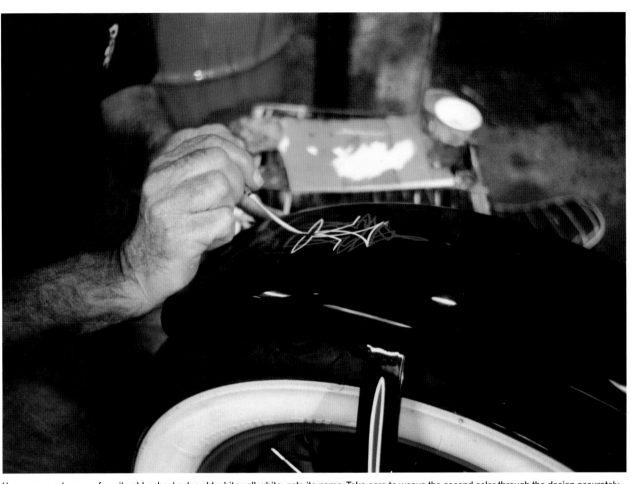

You can see where my favorite old-school color, old whitewall white, gets its name. Take care to weave the second color through the design accurately.

The red is mixed to match the red rim exactly and, in this case, is striped first. The white is used more as an accent. There is so much to the designs that I had to be careful not to make it too busy.

Of course, you need a flying eyeball to finish the nostalgic look of this nicely built bike—and a good, strong back to ride this hardtail.

Old-school deep red and gray are pretty typical on a black-suede paint job, but here I added some glossy black for an interesting and subtle touch.

Traditional stripes are turned into a simple eagle head accented with some quick lettering. This tank was striped in 1-Shot enamels with hardener added so it could be clear-coated with an automotive urethane

Pinstripe flames are always a hit. This mellow monotone job was done to suit the customer's taste. I used tape to roughly lay out the flames and followed the tape with the brush.

This simple three-color job looks like there is a lot more going on than there is because the designs are elongated to cover a larger area.

Motorcycle accessories can give you an opportunity to make a little more money by striping them to match the rest of the bike. A stretched teardrop motif with a blended fade to match the colors on the bike made this trailer look like it is part of a complete custom package.

Above left: Russ Mowry specializes in motorcycle striping. You will see him performing his magic all over the country at major bike rallies like Sturgis. Here, he demonstrates a simple design that he creates in five minutes with roughly 12 strokes of the brush.

Above right: Using this simple but effective design, Russ can complete an average striping job on a bike in less than a half an hour.

Right: Here is the design on a tank. Note the use of color. By starting on the inside of the design with the brightest color, he makes the design blend into the area.

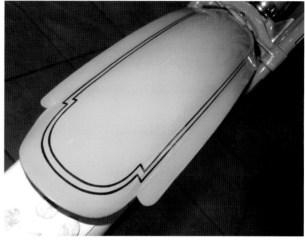

Above: Notice how delicately the classic fine lines were painted with sharp, crisp corners. Whoever striped this did a superb job on a beautiful restoration.

Left: Here's Russ Mowry's same basic motorcycle design as shown on the preceding page on a fender. Small changes keep it simple and clean. Working a major bike event, like Sturgis, you need to crank out the work while maintaining your quality.

Above and right: This old-school black-suede paint looks great with a clean design. The extra-glossy black adds subtle details.

CHAPTER 11
FLAMES AND SPECIAL EFFECTS

Nothing says "hot rod" like a good set of flames. I have jazzed up many a used car to try to help it sell, and painted flames can make a sale like nobody's business.

OUTLINE A TRADITIONAL FLAME JOB

After unmasking a traditional set of flames, you may notice how lame they look without outlines. They're like a person going out on the town half-dressed. There should be a law about this sort of indecent exposure. The outline is the touch that pulls the flames together and it was first used as a catchall for a poor masking job (and there were plenty of those). The new, more flexible tapes have made a world of difference in taping out basic flames.

Color choice is always critical, too. If the flames are traditional old school, they need a blue or white outline to be all dressed up. More modern-colored vehicles need to have an equally modern color to make them fit the nontraditional character of the car.

The traditional flame job beginning on page 138 illustrates how much an outline can change and enhance the look. Follow along though this step-by-step process so you will be familiar with this technique. If you have the opportunity to do a job like this, keep a record of your time to help you better estimate the next job. Keeping track of your time on any type of pinstriping will give you a gauge that can help you determine your hourly wage.

CREATE PINSTRIPE FLAMES

There are many variations on flames, such as the popular "real fire" that Mike Lavallee paints so well, but we are not

This flame job took a lot longer than I had figured it would take. The customer wanted to flame just the hood and front fenders, but the flames needed to be longer because of the car's massive size. The traditional light-blue outlining also took a lot more time. Fortunately, the customer was gracious and understanding with the larger bill.

This customer hated the color on this car he brought. Rather than repainting the entire car, he had me flame it to try and transform it. The outline helped move the color to the purple side of the spectrum.

Sometimes you can incorporate flames into a pinstripe graphic. Here, I started with a double stripe that got wider at the rear. Speaking of rears, this 1947 Dodge has a good-sized one. I switched from a striping brush to a quill and brushed the flame, airbrushed a fade, and outlined them both.

going to delve into that area or those tools here. We are going to remain focused on flames that can be painted with help from our friends the squirrels—well with their hair, anyway.

Pinstripe flames can be adapted to the end of a simple double stripe in a variety of styles, sizes, and shapes. Pinstripe flames can be as large as a full flame job, filling the entire car with just the outline. Pinstripe flames can be blended and overlapped together by striping over the first stripe at the tips with a lighter color and again with an even lighter color to make them pop.

A small, or "mini-flame", style flame can be painted or filled in solid with a lettering quill, then outlined with a pinstripe. These solid mini-flames look great with an airbrushed blend or highlight added to give a more traditional effect.

You can also tape out and mask a small flame design, brush in a pearl color, and "bag it" with plastic wrap, laying the plastic over the wet paint and then removing it to create a marbled effect. Here, again, you are only limited by your imagination.

continued on page 143

This little flame was not as involved as it may look. First I painted the light-orange base with a quill, followed by a darker red airbrush blend at one end and a white blend at the other end. Then I outlined it.

Outlining makes for a remarkable improvement to a flame job, no matter how big or small. The technique remains the same: start at the top and work down to avoid dragging your hand in the wet paint.

Here is how a traditional flame job looks after the masking is removed. The first step is to sand the edge with 1200-grit wet-dry sandpaper. This will make the edge smoother so the brush does not "track" unevenly when it is striped.

After the edge is sanded, it is buffed so there are no scratches left from the sanding. I begin the pinstriping at the top of the hood on the driver's side by leaning over from the passenger side of the car.

Standing on the passenger side and working from my farthest reach toward me, I can reach most everything on the top of the driver's side hood. Starting at the highest part of the hood nearest the cowl allows you to work downward and away from the wet paint.

After finishing off the outlining on the driver's side hood top, I move back to the passenger side and stripe the farthest flames first. Before I began the flame outline, I painted some black teardrops and shapes that I outlined later. This gives a little time for the teardrops to dry before they are outlined.

I continued on the passenger side, working toward me, and ending my stripes at the round inside sharp turns of the flames.

I pull the next stripe toward me in the same manner and intersect it with the previous stripe at the round inside sharp turns of the flames.

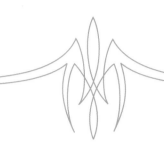

I continue downward to end at the bottom edge of the hood, finding a comfortable seat on the way. Days like this, working outside makes me glad to be alive. Then the hood sides are outlined.

After I finish all the outlining on the hood sides, I turn my attention to the other designs at the lower areas.

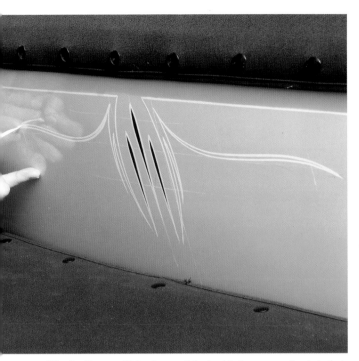

After the flame-outlining is complete, I get to have some fun. I start at the rear of the cab, between the top and the box cover, as it is the highest and most difficult to reach.

Two simple teardrops at the rear and sides are outlined; then I outline the Ford logo with my new series Exteme Liner brush from The Mack Brush Company.

This finishes off the rear with the simple two-color theme. Next, we move back to the front.

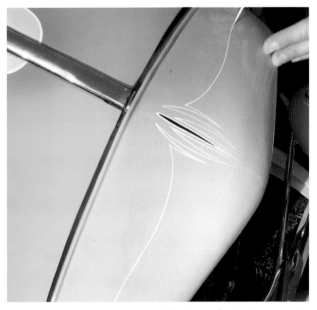

I like to do the harder-to-reach and difficult parts first so I can save the finishing touches for dessert. The last part to be striped is usually the grille shell. Then I walk around to make sure everything has been finished before I wash out my brush.

I forgot to do this spot on the top of the front cowl before I outlined the flame, so I had to be careful not to touch the wet paint all around me.

As I made the walk-around inspection, I realized the dashboard needed some striping to carry the theme throughout the car.

Here it sits, looking like it came out of one of those "little hot rod books" from the 1950s. I should have striped the wheels. Oh well . . . there will be others.

continued from page 137

You can even get a three-dimensional look by using two shades of a color, one a shade or two lighter than the other.

The following are a few examples of the different types of flames you can try. Use these suggestions to stimulate your own creative juices and bring about some new ideas of your own. Don't be afraid to try something you have never seen—after all, people always are asking for something different.

ADDING ELEMENTS

Dressing up your striping designs can make a personal statement about the car and owner. Customizing is all about giving a car that personal touch that expresses the owner's tastes and attitude. As I mentioned in Chapter 10, getting to know your customer and his or her car can spark creative ideas that make a striping design special.

Up to this point in this book we have focused on only one particular brush because we have talked mostly about traditional pinstriping. In fact, pinstriping brushes are only one style of brush and are specifically made to hold an enormous amount of paint so they can carry it a long distance. But, just as you have learned the four elements to handle the striping brush (grip, pressure, speed, and angle), you will need to learn how to use other brushes to add extra elements to your pinstriping designs.

Most of the following effects are not too difficult to execute. Just practice with any brush and you will soon see what it and you are capable of.

1948 TUCKER GOLD-LEAF STRIPE

It was an honor to work on this incredible work of art by the father and son team Bob and Rob Ida of Morganville, New Jersey. This hand-built custom was started from a rough fiberglass mold used in the movie Tucker. *Only 51 original Tuckers were ever built by Preston Tucker's company before it collapsed under the attack of politicians.*

To smooth out the discrepancy in the tone edge I use 3/8-inch tape as a layout guideline. Next, I tape right next to the guide tape with 1/4-inch The EDGE tape from Finesse Pinstriping. Applied correctly, this tape never bleeds through. After the 3/8-inch tape is removed, I brushed 1-Shot Fast Dry Gold Size with a few drops of white added to make it more opaque so I can see that I've covered the stripe. Notice I have left the 1/4-inch tape behind as a guide for the outline stripes to be painted later.

Gold size takes about an hour to set up, depending on the weather. I next apply the 23-karat patent gold leaf to the stripe, taking care to leave no holes, known as *holidays*.

The gold is gently taped with the heel of my hand to seat it in place.

This process of seating the gold with the heel of the hand picks up loose gold and distributes it to any places I may have overlooked.

With the gold down, I burnish it by delicately rubbing right to left with surgical cotton, followed by blowing off all the excess gold with all the doors in the shop open so that no loose pieces can get stuck to the outline stripes.

The gold can be engine-turned by hand or very carefully with a drill. Here, I use a turner I made out of a bolt covered with foam rubber, cotton, and velvet.

After the gold is engine-turned it's time to clear-coat the gold with a 1-Shot tinting clear that has a few drops of hardener added for strength.

The next day I stripe the edge of the gold in a rich, burnt-pumpkin orange using a Mack Fast-Lite size 2 striping brush.

Out in the sun you can see how the gold leaf and the outline color pop to life.

A rear view of the finished product.

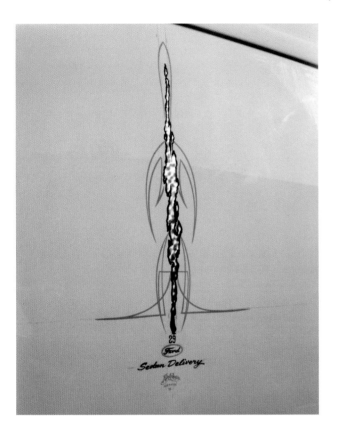

Above: Bill Beckner is a master at the art of gold leaf. Here he uses a roller applicator to lay down the gold on an antique fire engine. We have worked and laughed together on many such jobs.

Left: My old pinhead buddy Bill Beckner says, "A gold-leaf job is a gold-leaf job, whether it's a little or a lot." I guess that is true—the end product is brilliant no matter what the size. This little silver leaf shred added a whole new dimension to this '29 sedan delivery.

Gold-leaf pinstriping is elegant when it is thinly outlined with a pinstripe. This car was extensively decorated over many long days.

FLAMES AND SPECIAL EFFECTS

Pinstripe flames can be effective when they are small. These flames were an extension of the car's double pinstripes. How that car got into this hot rod show, I'll never know.

Pinstripe flames that are striped in two tones of the same color can give a three-dimensional appearance. Depending on where the lighter color is placed, they look either raised or cut in.

A simple graphic in pearl is highlighted with a pinstripe-into-flame design on this '34 Ford.

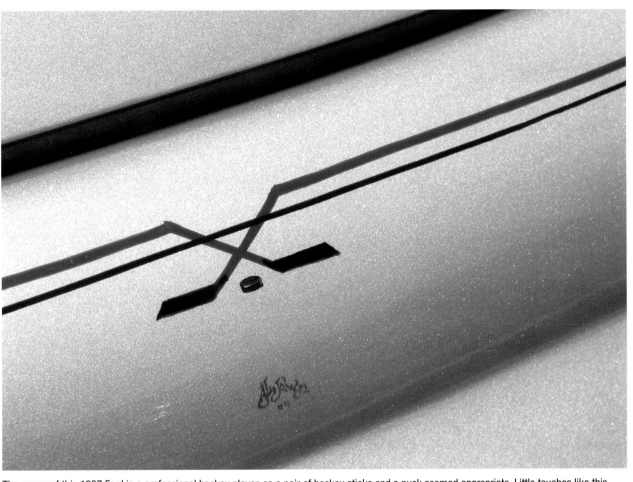

The owner of this 1937 Ford is a professional hockey player, so a pair of hockey sticks and a puck seemed appropriate. Little touches like this make a unique personal statement.

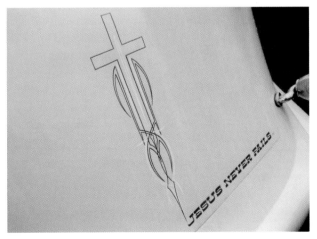

Adding a cross to the pinstriping design leads the viewer into the lettered message, which completes the theme on this sedan delivery.

A simple element added to the pinstriping design gives this Impala special interest and identity.

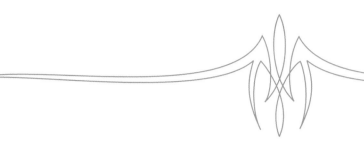

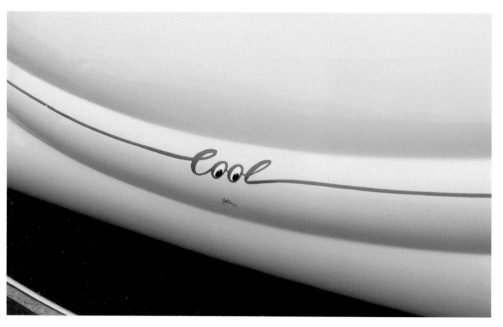

Here, the Mr. Horsepower logo leads off the stripe in flames. At the rear of the vehicle, the word "Cool" with a set of mooneyes completes the nostalgic look.

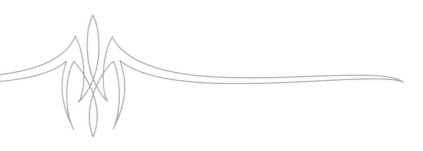

A musical note always works well around the antenna for a nostalgic 1950s motif. This is a black suede Ranchero.

A faux stone or marble effect can be created a number of ways. This one was done with a brush then highlighted and shadowed. "Like a Rock" rocks on this Chevy truck.

Another way to imitate a marble effect is to mask out a portion of a design then mix some pearl powder into some clear. Dip a wrinkled piece of plastic into the mixture and create some wild special effects.

Pearl powder added to clear can also be brushed into a taped-out stripe. Plastic wrap is simply laid over it to achieve a striking marble effect.

CHAPTER 12
INSPIRATION

It is quite natural to experience times where your work becomes "same ol' same ol'." The high pressure in this business can lead you to overuse some ideas or techniques from your bag of tricks that are sure to work. So where do you find water during these creative droughts? If you have young children around, I've found it to be inspiring to observe kids paint or draw. I love to listen to their conversations and storytelling; everything is new to a child.

Inspiration can be as simple as taking a break and going for a walk. Just look around: if you open your eyes and mind, new ideas can be found in places you least expect to find them.

You can get back in gear by looking at books, magazines, videos, and websites on the art of pinstriping, hot rods, kustom culture, signs, and automotive graphics and history. Also check out interesting resources on topics such as ornamental design, Art Deco, Art Nouveau, and carriage-painting and decoration.

Strolling though car and motorcycle shows is always a good way to observe the varied styles and techniques of pinstriping designs.

Art exhibits, galleries, tattoo studios, skateparks, packaging at the supermarket, and even graffiti on buildings—the list is as big as your imagination. Sometimes you just need to jump start it.

Of course, if you have never gone to a pinhead panel jam, you're really missing out. It's hard to describe the incredibly friendly atmosphere at these creativity meets. One

Spending a day or two at a major car show will give you plenty of inspiration. Study hundreds of cars from all over the country and the multitude of paint styles and techniques. The annual Grand National Roadster Show in Pomona, California, hosts the country's best of the best.

I had many opportunities to stripe cars with host Pekka Mannermaa and others at the Grand Stripe-O-Rama in Finland in 2006. It was a joyful experience, "panel jamming" with the "Arctic pinheads" . . . a true international exchange program of ideas and inspiration.

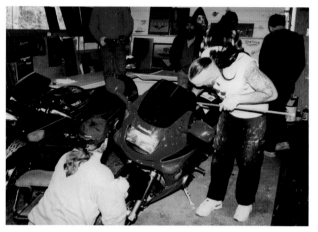

You might want to get in on a group project like this bike jam with Mike Lavallee and Glen Weisgerber. You can find a get-together in your area if you seek them out. Check the web sites and magazines for listings and get involved. Where else will you find this one-on-one type of education?

can work next to artists from all over the world. A panel jam is like a music jam session—free-form, mass sharing of ideas and techniques. "I'm not good enough to work with them," you may say. Sorry. There are no ego problems here—everyone is there to share.

These events take place all over the country and are spreading all over the world as well. You can find different meets listed on the web and in the trade magazines (see: "Web Links and Sources"). I always leave these meets with something new and with my imagination supercharged. You will never get as much free information anywhere else, so I'll see you at the next event, OK?

You can also get one-on-one training at "pinstripe boot camps," at two- and three-day weekend workshops usually in small groups.

Try new color combinations that you usually would not use. When I've been stumped I've asked my wife to suggest a color combination and have always been delighted with the result. Play—yes, play—with other styles you've never tried before. Painting with a new technique can turn into an exploration to uncharted territory. I have discovered many new ideas totally by mistake. One time, I had finished a graphic on a pickup truck when the plastic I was using for masking blew into the wet paint. After whining and getting upset, I looked at the patterns left behind by the plastic. I realized that it looked pretty cool, so I continued the effect

on the rest of the graphic. I've used that trick to death. I guess it's time for another happy accident.

We are constantly being bombarded by input from everywhere, whether we like or not. I call this the "Route 22 Effect." Old Highway 22 runs east to west though central New Jersey, with signs about every 100 feet. Each sign is

Questions and answers are batted around in an ego-free environment inside the Bullpen at the USSC Sign World trade show in Atlantic City, New Jersey, every December. You may work with pro stripers like Mike Z, Mr. J, Howie, and others on a panel jam like this one.

INSPIRATION

Pinhead boot camps offer individual training over a two- or three-day weekend course. These smaller groups focus on specific points of interest and technique.

bigger and brighter than the last, all trying to grab your attention. After a while your senses just shut down from this visual overload. Desensitized you can cope, but at what price? Your mind blocks out all details to quiet the visual noise.

Quiet is a luxury that can be hard to find in our high-speed world. When you do find this peace, it can be an enlightening experience. Many captivating sounds are overlooked in society's mad velocity. The new arrivals of nature that fill the air with song every season are there to inspire you. Turn off the radio or whatever other noise is in your workplace and get a perspective you may be lacking. Slow down and smell the roses, as they say. Can you remember how many senses we have been gifted with?

Music is another form of expression that can be inspiring or debilitating. Try changing your musical diet to see how it affects your creativity. It is virtually impossible to be inspired to stripe an elegantly restored Deusenberg with any exactness with screaming, head-banging "music" blaring at you! In such an instance, definitely try classical!

But if you need to find the best way out of the desert, ask the Creator for direction. He will quench your thirst during these droughts—you only need to ask.

Maintain,

AJ

Pinheads Jack Giachino and Brando attempt to add some stripes on Paul Martin. These pinhead events are not only educational; they are full of fun and craziness.

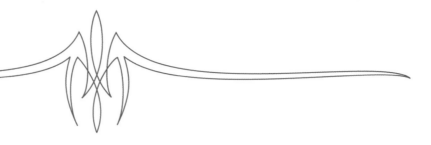

WEB LINKS AND SOURCES

1-Shot Paint, www.1shot.com
Alan Johnson Grafix, www.alanjohnsongrafix.com
The American Hot Rod Foundation, www.ahrf.com
The Astragal Press, www.astragalpress.com
Auto Art Magazine, www.autoartmagazine.com
Auto Graphics Magazine, www.nbm.com
Custom Auto, www.realhotrods.com
Don Garlits Museum of Drag Racing, www.garlits.com
Hand Lettering Forum, www.handletteringforum.com
Hibernia Auto Restorations, www.hiberniaautorestorers.com
Hotrod & Restoration Magazine, www.hotrodshow.com
Ida Automotive, www.idaautomotive.com
The Jalopy Journal, www.jalopyjournal.com
Juxtapoz Magazine, www.juxtapoz.com
Kustom Shop, www.kustomshop.com
Letterville: The Letterhead Website, www.letterhead.com
Mack Brush Company, www.mackbrush.com
A Magazine About Letterheads, www.letterheadmagazine.com
Museum of Transportation, www.forneymuseum.com

NHRA Motorsports Museum, www.museum.nhra.com/
North Jersey Street Rod Association, www.njsra.com
Petersen Automotive Museum, www.petersen.org
Phoenix Auto Restorations,
   www.phoenixrodandcustom.com
Polycracker, Inc., www.thomasnet.com
Radir Wheels and Tire, www.radirwheels.com
The Razorbacks, www.razorbacksmusic.com
Rod & Custom Magazine, www.primedia.com
The Rodders Journal, www.roddersjournal.com
Saral Paper Corporation, www.saralpaper.com
Schwan-STABILO, www.stabilo.com
Sign Business Magazine, www.nbm.com
SignCraft Magazine, www.signcraft.com
Stone Barn Automobile Restoration,
   www.stonebarnclassiccars.com
T. J. Ronan paint Corp., www.ronanpaint.com
XOTIC Colours, www.xoticcolours.com
Xcaliber Brushes, www.xcaliberart.com

INDEX

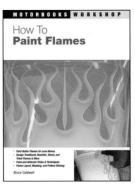

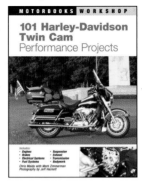
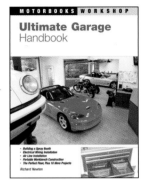